T0248239

## Praise for Aaron J. Leonard

"*Heavy Radicals* is a concise and insightful history of a long-forgotten but vibrant radical movement. Leonard and Gallagher break new ground in revealing the extent to which law enforcement will go to infiltrate, destabilize and ultimately destroy domestic political organizations that espouse a philosophy counter to the status quo. To better understand the current state of domestic surveillance and political repression, from Occupy Wall Street to the Edward Snowden revelations, start with this little gem of a book."

—T. J. English, author of *The Savage City:*
*Race, Murder, and a Generation on the Edge* and
*Havana Nocturne: How the Mob Owned*
*Cuba . . . and Then Lost It to the Revolution*

"In this masterfully written and extensively researched book, Aaron Leonard with Conor A. Gallagher offers a no-nonsense critical analysis of one of the most resilient, misunderstood, and controversial anti-capitalist organizations of the last fifty years. This book is a MUST READ for anyone invested in nuancing their understanding of revolutionary political struggle and unrelenting state repression in the United States."

—Robeson Taj Frazier, author of *The East Is Black:*
*Cold War China in the Black Radical Imagination*

"Maoists, dedicated to revolutionary class struggle, the RCP was one of many organizations that fought to carry on the 60s struggle for radical change in the United States well after SDS and other more well-known groups imploded. Leonard and Gallagher help us to understand how the RCP's revolutionary ideology resonated with a small group of young people in post-1968 America, took inspiration from the People's Republic of China, and brought down the wrath of the FBI."

—David Farber, author of *The Age of Great Dreams:*
*America in the 1960s*

"Meticulously researched, drawing on both internal documents hiding in plain sight and a wealth of information gained through laborious freedom of information requests, *Heavy Radicals* is a great example of history of the near past—in examining how the FBI acted, we are better able to understand the methods employed in undermining dissent today."

—Eveline Lubbers, author of *Secret Manoeuvres in the Dark: Corporate and Police Spying on Activists*

"*A Threat of the First Magnitude* reveals in graphic detail the extent that activists and citizens in the leftist movements of the Sixties and Seventies were manipulated by the FBI via informants they believed to be trusted friends. More importantly, it reveals how little the FBI cares about the individuals whose lives they ruin in the name of national security . . . a riveting story of FBI lies and deceit. It is a fascinating history that is also a prescient warning. After reading this book, I can't help but wonder how things might have turned out if the government's informants had never been members of the groups they helped destroy."

—Ron Jacobs, author of *The Way the Wind Blew: A History of the Weather Underground* and *Daydream Sunset: The 60s Counterculture in the 70s*

"We already knew the FBI spied on 'political subversives.' Now Leonard and Gallagher turn a welcome spotlight on the informants who infiltrated deeply—and likely illegally—into radical political groups."

—Scott Martelle, author of *Blood Passion: The Ludlow Massacre and Class War in the American West* and *The Fear Within: Spies, Commies, and American Democracy on Trial*

"Those interested in political surveillance but not the contours of American Maoism might question the utility of a study with such an intense focus on the RU/RCP. But as Leonard and Gallagher

correctly point out, when it comes to FBI political surveillance, groups like the RU/RCP are "where the bodies are buried."
—Chip Gibbons, *Jacobin*

"Aaron Leonard's copious and impeccable research uncovers how and why American icons like Woody Guthrie became targets of America's secret police: the FBI. More than that, Leonard's critical analysis helps us understand the impact on music, social movements, and indeed society as a whole, of both the folk singers and the bureau. *The Folksingers and the Bureau* is a must-read for music lovers and defenders of civil liberties alike."
—Mat Callahan, author of *The Trouble with Music*

"A fascinating understanding of the beginnings of the folk music revival through the lens of the particularly zealous FBI. A groundbreaking approach to the post-World War II destructive Red Scare and the numerous folk musicians who were targeted."
—Ronald D. Cohen, author of *Roots of the Revival: American and British Folk Music in the 1950s* and *Rainbow Quest: The Folk Music Revival and American Society*

"A valuable and timely study, with new evidence and insights suited to our present moment. Leonard balances primary evidence and secondary source knowledge with deft storytelling. Ultimately, he shows that the image of FBI agents trailing folkies with banjos is no laughing matter. The federal suppression of folk artists should be taken as deadly serious and fits into a broader context of repression generally as an ongoing norm in U.S. life."
—Steven Garabedian, associate professor of history, Marist College

"Folk singers have long been America's canaries in the coal mine, singing out danger, singing out warning, singing out love. To examine why a small band of warblers were able to strike such terror into the heart of the FBI, Leonard has delved into the files, many of them never before seen. Historically informed and impressively contextualized, *The Folksinger and the Bureau* is a dark tale of persecution, paranoia, and valiant resistance to tyranny."

—Will Kaufman, author of *Woody Guthrie, American Radical* and *Mapping Woody Guthrie*

"With his previous two books—*Heavy Radicals* and *A Threat of the First Magnitude*, both coauthored with Conor Gallagher—Leonard has proven his ability to craft a compelling story from the records of political repression. . . . In focusing on the repression of radical folk musicians in the mid-twentieth century, Leonard adds a new dimension."

—Alexander Billet, *Jacobin*

"Aaron J. Leonard is a most unusual writer. He scrutinizes the files of repressive (supposedly investigative) government agencies—a veritable treasure trove of false accusations of disloyalty and potential subversion."

—Paul Buhle, *Truthout*

"Leonard has established himself as a leading expert when it comes to accessing and researching FBI files. [In *Whole World in an Uproar*] he deftly sorts through these documents to demonstrate the breadth of state surveillance against musicians who offended those in power."

—Scott Costen, *Morning Star* (UK)

"What happened when HUAC, the FBI, Jim Crow, corporate media outlets, drug warriors, the religious right, and even the Old Left tried to stop a freight train? Drawing on a broad range of sources, including FBI files, *Whole World in an Uproar* recounts that momentous story."

—Peter Richardson, author of *No Simple Highway: A Cultural History of the Grateful Dead*

"Aaron Leonard integrates an amazing amount of research into [*Whole World in an Uproar*] that ranges from FBI surveillance of the Old Left to the rock scene to the social dissension around the anti-Vietnam War and Black liberation movements. A well-thought-through, fascinating documentary about movements and people who were affected by oppressive societal actions."

—Terri Thal, former manager of Dave Van Ronk and Bob Dylan

"[*Whole World in an Uproar* is a] fascinating counter-history of the 1960s music revolution through the eyes of the persecutors, paranoiacs, and culture warriors who tried to stop it."

—Dorian Lynskey, author of *33 Revolutions Per Minute: A History of Protest Songs*

**Meltdown Expected**

# Meltdown Expected

## Crisis, Disorder, and Upheaval at the End of the 1970s

AARON J. LEONARD

**Rutgers University Press**

New Brunswick, Camden, and Newark, New Jersey

London and Oxford

Rutgers University Press is a department of Rutgers, The State University of New Jersey, one of the leading public research universities in the nation. By publishing worldwide, it furthers the University's mission of dedication to excellence in teaching, scholarship, research, and clinical care.

Library of Congress Cataloging-in-Publication Data

Names: Leonard, Aaron J., author.
Title: Meltdown expected : crisis, disorder, and upheaval at the end of the 1970s / Aaron J. Leonard.
Description: New Brunswick, New Jersey : Rutgers University Press, [2024] | Includes bibliographical references and index.
Identifiers: LCCN 2023038712 | ISBN 9781978836464 (cloth) | ISBN 9781978836471 (epub) | ISBN 9781978836488 (pdf)
Subjects: LCSH: United States—Civilization—1970– | United States— History—1969– | Nineteen seventies. | United States—Politics and government—1977–1981. | United States—Economic conditions—1971–1981. | BISAC: HISTORY / United States / 20th Century | POLITICAL SCIENCE / History & Theory
Classification: LCC E169.12 .L4475 2023 | DDC 973.926—dc23/eng/20240117
LC record available at https://lccn.loc.gov/2023038712

A British Cataloging-in-Publication record for this book is available from the British Library.

⊖ The paper used in this publication meets the requirements of the American National Standard for Information Sciences—Permanence of Paper for Printed Library Materials, ANSI Z39.48-1992.

rutgersuniversitypress.org

For Terry, Sally, and Robin

# Contents

# Preface

I admit to being at a loss when I finished my previous book and considered what to focus on next. I wanted to write a history but also wanted to move beyond my previous two books *The Folk Singers and the Bureau* and *Whole World in an Uproar*. Those titles, which traveled the distance from 1940 to 1972, had a particular center of attention on repression. Given that, and what I had written before then on U.S. Maoism and the Federal Bureau of Investigation, I wanted to get away from that more singular focus. In mulling this over I got to thinking about the period in recent history that has been less examined, a time that was also among the most consequential in my life. In doing that, certain things started to come together.

In the years 1976 to 1979, I was a dedicated political activist working with a group that would go from organizing among the working class—with a long view toward revolutionary socialism—to, by the decade's end, pursuing a course based on the view that the prospect of revolution was a possibility in the near term. Putting aside the soundness of either analysis, it was nonetheless a long trip in a short space of time. As such, it led to my moving around a fair amount—often finding myself in the middle of significant events.

In 1976 I was nineteen years old and living in Tacoma, Washington, where I worked at a food processing plant. At first, I worked on the pickle production line—pushing errant pickles into the jars ceaselessly streaming past me and the other young people working a summer job. Taken on permanently, I was dispatched to the factory's canned chili plant. There I was tasked with pouring a multi-gallon tub of cooked ground beef into a vat of hot chili sauce. One had to be careful in this: my workmate and I needed to proceed with caution when tipping the meat into the cauldron so as not to have scalding sauce splash back into our faces. My political friends called this firsthand experience with socialized production. I called it a conspiracy to make me an arthritic burn case before reaching the age of thirty. This was in the heart of the "malaise" of the 1970s—and I distinctly recall falling asleep as Jimmy Carter gave his fireside chat on energy. That period, I have come to understand, was a far shorter one than historic memory suggests.

In late 1977 I moved from Tacoma to Seattle, where I would work with food in a different capacity. Having been asked by my comrades to "organize youth," I got a job in a burger joint—this at the Campbell's Soup franchise called Herfy's—home of their grandly named Hefty Burger. While I was working away, and not being too successful in organizing youth toward revolutionary communism, changes were underway globally that would upend the relative stability I had found in the Pacific Northwest.

With the death of Mao Zedong in 1976, the group I worked with, the Revolutionary Communist Party (RCP), and its affiliated organizations, found itself in crisis. The RCP was a U.S. Maoist group, and its model, the People's Republic of China, was systematically moving away from the radical tenets of Maoism toward something they came to call socialism with Chinese characteristics—that is, capitalism operating within a nominal socialist shell. As a result, there would be a schism in the group, with my soon-to-be former comrades in the Northeast and parts of the Midwest leaving to form another entity. As a result, in March 1978 I was asked to move to New York City with some other comrades to re-establish a political presence for the RCP by way of its youth organization the Revolutionary Communist Youth Brigade.

These were eventful times in New York—the city was shaken by the flight of industry, fiscal crisis, and general degeneration, in this onetime showcase of U.S. postwar affluence. There was also an incubating political tumult. In New York, I marched with Iranian students against the regime of the Shah, protested against police violence, and worked to support the independence movement underway in Zimbabwe.

As things developed, my stay in New York was brief. In August 1978, I moved to Philadelphia—this two weeks after the confrontation in the Powelton Village neighborhood between the Philadelphia police and the polarizing Black communal organization MOVE. A few weeks before my arrival, police had a standoff with MOVE, and one of their officers was killed. I was astonished as a friend took me on a walking tour of the city to discover that police had razed the house where MOVE had lived, leaving nothing but an empty lot. That action preceded the trial later that year of nine MOVE members accused of responsibility for killing the officer—something the group claimed was a result of friendly fire.[1]

Of note too, it was in Philly that I first heard the Black journalist Mumia Abu Jamal, who would later join the MOVE organization. At the time he was still a correspondent on the local NPR station—his trial and incarceration for his conviction for killing of another Philadelphia police officer was still a couple of years in the future.

Ensconced in Philadelphia—mainly doing political work at Temple University—in January 1979, I traveled to Washington, DC, to confront Deng Xiaoping on his historic visit to the United States. While there I was arrested in the course of the RCP's "Committee for a Fitting Welcome" demonstration, aimed at denouncing the Chinese leader as an anti-Maoist revisionist. I had been at the front of the march, unaware that behind me some comrades had a brief, but violent, encounter with police. While I missed that, and because I was fired up and "in the moment," I returned to the remains of the march and began to rail against the police. They responded by beating me to the ground and arresting me. At the time I saw my arrest as being part of something important. However, facing a felony assault on a police officer charge, with the potential of five years in prison, was, to put it mildly, sobering. Luckily, in my case the government ended up dropping charges. Unfortunately, I did not draw the correct conclusion that the organization I was aligned with was operating with a skewed understanding of reality and that I should therefore disassociate myself from it. It would be many years before I did so. Hindsight, as they say, is crystal clear.

Back in Philly, I would, with millions of others, confront the prospect of radioactive fallout from Three Mile Island, ninety miles to the west in Middletown, Pennsylvania. And I was back in DC in November when Iranian students seized the U.S. embassy in Teheran and squared off against raging anti-Iranian students on the American University campus.

Oh, and I should add, I also got to see the Clash, still in their punk phase, perform at Philadelphia's Walnut Street Theater on their first-ever U.S. tour. This is thanks to a ticket—fifth-row center—given to me by a workmate at the Wawa convenience store on the Penn campus. The concert took place the evening after the group had performed their historic shows at New York's Palladium, during which Paul Simonon had wielded his bass like an axe and smashed it into the stage floor.

There were other undertakings, some more dubious than others. Regardless, looking back it feels like in 1978 and 1979, I was where I should have been—if not always doing the things I was doing. That said, my personal experience—as rich and thrilling as it was at times—was limited by the myopia of my political dogmatism and constraints of what one person can discern when wholly in the midst of things. Being there was not the same as understanding where I was.

In that regard, the central question in undertaking this project is: Why was so much happening? What was it about the final months of the seventies that made them so different than the years that preceded them? Or put another way, why was it that so much historical activity was packed into such a small period of time? While it was not tumult on the level of the sixties, events such as the revolutions in Iran and Nicaragua and the civil war in El Salvador suggested that we were entering a sustained period of upsurge. Of course, that was not the case. Rather, in hindsight, it is clear that the central contradictions globally were shifting toward the concluding events of the Cold War. Nonetheless, getting a grip on the what, where, and why of it all turned out to be the story I wanted to tell.

# Abbreviations

| | |
|---|---|
| BLA | Black Liberation Army |
| BPP | Black Panther Party |
| CIA | Central Intelligence Agency |
| COINTELPRO | Counterintelligence Program |
| CPD | Chicago Police Department |
| CPUSA | Communist Party USA |
| CWP | Communist Workers Party |
| ERA | Equal Rights Amendment |
| FBI | Federal Bureau of Investigation |
| FEMA | Federal Emergency Management Agency |
| FISA | Foreign Intelligence Surveillance Act |
| FISC | Foreign Intelligence Surveillance Court |
| FMLN | Farabundo Martí National Liberation Front (El Salvador) |
| GPCR | Great Proletarian Cultural Revolution |
| ICBM | intercontinental ballistic missile |
| IRA | Irish Republican Army |
| ISA | Iranian Students Association |
| MIA | Marxists Internet Archive |

| | |
|---|---|
| NATO | North Atlantic Treaty Organization |
| NPR | National Public Radio |
| NRC | Nuclear Regulatory Committee |
| NSC | National Security Council |
| NYPD | New York Police Department |
| OAPEC | Organization of Arab Petroleum Exporting Countries |
| PDPA | People's Democratic Party of Afghanistan |
| PFOC | Prairie Fire Organizing Committee |
| PLO | People's Law Office |
| RAR | Rock Against Racism |
| RCP | Revolutionary Communist Party |
| RNA | Republic of New Afrika |
| SAC | Special Agent in Charge |
| SALT I & II | Strategic Arms Limitation Talks |
| SAVAK | Sazman-e Etelaat Va Amniat Keshvar (Iran) |
| TMI | Three Mile Island |
| WUO | Weather Underground Organization |
| WVO | Workers Viewpoint Organization |

**Meltdown Expected**

# Introduction

New Year's 1978 in the United States was not especially eventful. In a roundup of the holiday, the *Washington Post* described it as "both carefully ushered in and routinely ignored."[1] That mundane assessment aside, the paper's opinion page was replete with forecasts and advice. Columnist Jack Anderson offered a piece full of divinations, both whimsical and grounded. Among his predictions, Egypt would invade Libya, the world's most active volcano, Mauna Loa in Hawai'i, would erupt, and the Senate would agree to ratify a nuclear weapons limitation treaty with the Soviet Union during the second round of the Strategic Arms Limitation Talks (SALT II).[2] None of this came to pass.

In a more advisory manner, "the dean of the Washington press corps" David Broder advised President Jimmy Carter to spend more time on domestic matters, cautioning him that "the Panamanians, the Palestinians, and the Politburo may look easier to deal with than the tax lobbyists, the energy conferees or the unemployed."[3] Another pundit, Joseph Kraft, offered the view that much like 1977 and 1978, "my impression is that the best that can be expected here and abroad is more of the same."[4]

Such august opinions belied major changes just around the corner. Had these pundits ventured out of their Washington Beltway comfort zone, they might have anticipated as much. The reality was that by the end of 1978, the United States was on track to sharply draw the curtain on the "Me Decade" as it hurdled into the final phase of the Cold War.

## The End of the Sixties

To understand why the period from late 1978 to 1979 was different from the seventies as a whole, it is helpful to break that decade down into constituent parts. Specifically, the decade is better understood as consisting of three periods: the end of the sixties, a seventies interlude, and the onset of the final phase of the Cold War.

The first years of the seventies were for all intents and purposes a continuation of the tumultuous sixties. The year 1970 saw the United States send troops across the border into Cambodia, sparking a wave of demonstrations on campuses across the country, including at Kent State in Ohio where four students would be shot dead by National Guardsmen deployed to counter the demonstrators. The largest anti-war demonstration to ever happen in the United States occurred in 1971, and protests continued throughout 1972. Beyond protests, was the prison uprising and its aftermath in Attica, in upstate New York, which occurred in the fall of 1971. Along with this, domestic radicals from the Black Panthers, the Yippies, and Weathermen continued to garner significant attention from authorities and media, while a core of the new left cohered into the Revolutionary Union, a pro-Chinese, Maoist organization. Others from that milieu were incubating their own organizational plans. Culturally, anti-establishment films such as *M.A.S.H.*, *Catch-22*, *Five Easy Pieces*, and others were circulating at the opening of the new decade, along with some of the most memorable music by artists such as John Lennon, the Rolling Stones, Marvin Gaye, and quite a few others.

It was not until January 1973 with the signing of the peace treaty with Vietnam, the de facto conclusion of the war for the United

States, that the 1960s fundamentally ended. While this would be an uneven transition, events had crossed the threshold into a new period.

## The Seventies Interlude

What followed was the period most have come to associate with the seventies. It was during this time that the U.S. population was digesting governmental mendacity surrounding the Vietnam War; Richard Nixon came under siege for his actions surrounding the Watergate break-in; and the Federal Bureau of Investigation (FBI) and the Central Intelligence Agency (CIA) were investigated for extralegal, illegal, and even murderous activity.

Culturally—despite a sixties sensibility still informing a good deal—there was a shift. Drug use went from consciousness-raising to escapism—the goal being getting wasted rather than high. Similarly, the experimental and communal aesthetic of music was giving way to a good degree of self-indulgence and gimmickry, with rock concerts changing from tribal gatherings to mega-events—at top dollar—in commercial stadiums.

On the radical activist front, there was retreat, confusion, and transformation. The anti-war movement, which had seen a goodly number of its leaders and activists become anti-imperialist, even revolutionary, ended. Some signaled surrender, prostrating themselves in front of the authorities, while a good many others shifted their focus. In the place of radical inclinations toward, if not overturning, at least questioning everything, were movements that had sprung to life in the previous decade, which were focused more on achievable rights within the standing order—from women's rights to Black empowerment to gay rights.

This occurred amid an unprecedented economic crisis. Not only was there the due bill for the Vietnam War, but a Middle East oil embargo—initiated in response to U.S. support of Israel in its war against Egypt in 1973—had also created an unprecedented energy crisis.[5] What followed was a recession, economic stagnation, and uncontrolled inflation. At the same time, accelerating deindustrialization and automation chipped away at the post–World War II order and the social contract that had been in place for a critical section of the U.S. working class.

All of this played out between 1973 and 1978. While the ruling forces of the United States tended to their wounds, the larger population struggled to get its bearings or sought escape. It would be a brief respite. By the end of 1978, matters shifted in a wholly different direction.

## Decade's End

One of the most important factors in the United States' extrication from Vietnam—which prevented things from coming more undone than they had—was the Nixon administration's rapprochement with China.[6] The reconciliation between the two countries meant the United States could leave Vietnam without taking the massive geopolitical strategic hit it would have had to absorb if it remained in open antagonism with both the Soviet Union and China. True, the Soviet Union would benefit from consolidated relations with the newly united Vietnam, but in the wake of Nixon's 1972 visit to Beijing, the United States no longer had to consider China an adversary.[7] The normalization of relations culminated in 1979 with Chinese premier Deng Xiaoping's visit to Washington and the official opening of a Chinese embassy. As such it represented a new geostrategic situation, one with immediate and long-term consequences.

While this was cause for celebration for the U.S. political class, it was offset by events in the Middle East. At the same moment Deng was meeting with Carter in Washington, millions of Iranians were in the streets in a revolution that would sweep the U.S.-backed Shah from power. Overnight this upended the status quo in this key region.

Further complicating matters, the United States confronted rising instability in Central America. First, in July 1979, the pro-U.S. dictator Anastasio Somoza Debayle of Nicaragua was forced to flee the country to avoid being overtaken by a leftist insurgency. That was soon followed by the onset of a civil war in nearby El Salvador.

Adding to this instability, the Soviet Union invaded Afghanistan in order to shore up its own geopolitical power. That move in turn was received as a gauntlet by the U.S. power structure, which would initiate a proxy war with the Soviets in Central Asia. While détente—the term of art signifying the de-escalation of conflict between the United States and the Soviet Union—had been the watchword mid-decade, by decade's end the term was quickly becoming an anachronism.

Beyond such geopolitical challenges was the abatement of measures toward domestic accountability and reform. During the middle of the decade, Congress had convened the Watergate Committee, the House committee to investigate the John F. Kennedy and Martin Luther King assassinations, and the Senate committee—known as the Church Committee—on U.S. intelligence gathering. By decade's end, however, concerns turned from exposure and reform toward acquitting and empowering—particularly the government's intelligence apparatus. The latter was on sharp display in what appeared on the surface to be a matter of accountability.

In April 1978, former FBI director L. Patrick Gray, associate director W. Mark Felt, and deputy assistant director Edward S. Miller were indicted for conspiring to violate the constitutional rights of U.S. citizens. Their alleged crime was, in their capacity as FBI managers, of facilitating "black bag jobs" (illegal break-ins) aimed at countering the political violence of radicals such as the Weathermen, as well as other domestic subversives. While the case suggested a continued reckoning, as it wound its way through the courts it transformed into measures complementary to re-empowering the FBI and other like organizations.

Meanwhile, the various radicals targeted confronted a far more hostile terrain in their efforts toward a transformative future. While most reconciled themselves to the situation, opting to undertake efforts toward reform, others doubled down, adopting moves aimed at keeping the fire of revolution burning—with, at times, tragic results.

Amid all this were rumblings in the realm of popular music. Where the seventies are notorious for stultifying culture—from the saccharine work of Debbie Boone to the inanity of the Captain & Tennille's "Muskrat Love"—by 1978–1979 artists such as the Ramones, Patti Smith, Bruce Springsteen, Gil Scott-Heron, Peter Tosh, Bob Marley, the Clash, and quite a few others were transforming the musical landscape. While this upsurge would, predictably, quickly be integrated into the mainstream where it could be capitalized on, for a moment it exerted a subversive force.

There were other significant, if less sensational, events. The United States and Panama signed a second treaty in 1978 meaning the U.S. would hand over control of the Panama Canal by 1999. And at Camp David in the fall of 1978, Jimmy Carter brokered a deal between Anwar Sadat and Menachem Begin, removing Egypt as a threat to Israel and making the latter a huge benefactor of U.S. military aid.[8] That event, however, which was heralded as a landmark of "peace" and garnered Begin and Sadat the Nobel Peace Prize, did not resolve the standing issues of the Palestinian people in the West Bank or Gaza Strip. As such, it ensured that conflict would continue.[9]

What follows is an effort to capture the multitude of forces and changes in play. To do this, rather than operating chronologically, things are presented thematically. While most of the events and actors in this period are accounted for, as with most things, it would be neither possible nor desirable to do a comprehensive recounting. That said, the aim is to show how the torpor of the 1970s was displaced by the crush of events in advance of the last phase of the Cold War.

# 1

# The Beginning
# of the End of
# the 1970s

There is all across our land a
growing sense of peace and
a sense of common purpose.

—PRESIDENT JIMMY CARTER,
January 19, 1978

In the fall of 1978, most thinking people taking stock of political
and cultural events in the United States could be forgiven for thinking that the haze of the 1970s was not likely to lift anytime soon.
Donna Summer was riding high on the charts with a disco version
of the surrealist heartbreak song "MacArthur Park"; the stoner
comedy *Up in Smoke* was riding "high" at the box office; and the
*Happy Days* spinoff *Laverne and Shirley*—the latest in a long line
of fifties nostalgia dating to *American Graffiti*—was the top

television show. In politics, the Democrats, who had held fast in the midterms, retained both houses, to work alongside Democratic president Jimmy Carter to undo the wreckage wrought by the Nixon administration. Globally, the Vietnam War, however tenuously, was fading into the past, and the United States and the Soviet Union seemed on track to hammer out constraints on nuclear weapons. The world, still convalescing from the calamities of the previous decade, seemed in no hurry to wake up from its relative repose.

Events in November 1978 would show this to be an illusion. First, on November 18, word came across the newswires of a mass homicide/suicide of 908 Americans—a third of them children—in Jonestown, Guyana. Eleven days later, in San Francisco, a disturbed right-wing politician gunned down two of his liberal colleagues in cold blood. This included the city's first openly gay elected official. And then there was Iran, where fury against the U.S.-backed Shah was escalating to a point beyond anything the wise heads in the U.S. State Department could control. All of this could be dismissed, however upsetting, as anomalous. But that would require an assumption that there would not be more to come, an assumption that would have been wrong.

## The End of a Socialist Paradise

They had come from all over the Bay Area to rally for the International Hotel, a building long past its prime but located on lucrative real estate in San Francisco's Chinatown. As such it was a target for redevelopment. Real estate compulsions or not, it was home to several score of elderly Filipino residents who would be made homeless by the city's plans.[1] For the residents and their considerable number of supporters, the move to tear down the "I Hotel" was a gauntlet and sparked a major effort to save the building. The height of resistance saw the residents' supporters surround the hotel on

Jim Jones at the International Hotel, San Francisco, 1977. Photo: Nancy Wong.

January 14, 1977—a demonstration that compelled a judge to issue a temporary stay on evictions. Among the estimated five thousand who took part in the demonstration were two thousand who had been organized by the chairman of the San Francisco Housing Authority.

That particular protest might have been cataloged as emblematic of one of several struggles of modest impact that occupied the space of the middle 1970s. However, the identity of the Housing Authority official tied it to something else. As it turned out, he was also an ordained minister. His name was Jim Jones and the demonstrators he brought to the I-Hotel were members of his Peoples Temple.[2]

The struggle at the I-Hotel was ultimately lost, with the city successful in evicting the last residents that summer. As for Jones, who was becoming increasingly paranoid about life in the United States, he began to look beyond the situation in San Francisco toward setting up a safe haven outside the country. As a result, he decamped his church to the South American country of Guyana.[3]

While Jones and his followers may have left the country, they would soon be thrust center stage in headlines worldwide.

On November 14, 1978, U.S. congressman Leo Ryan, who represented the 11th Congressional District that covered an area to the east of San Francisco, traveled to Guyana, the only English-speaking country in South America. He made the trip in order to investigate reports that people in Jim Jones's church, which had created a settlement in the dense Guyanese jungle, were being held against their will.

Ryan was accompanied by an entourage that included two staff members, an NBC newsman, his two crew members, three print journalists from San Francisco and another from the *Washington Post*, and four members of a group called Concerned Relatives— family members and advocates for those living in Jonestown.[4] Also traveling with Ryan were attorneys Mark Lane—a famous John F. Kennedy conspiracy theorist—and Charles Garry, the radical attorney who had represented Black Panther leaders Bobby Seale and Huey P. Newton. The lawyers had been hired by Jim Jones.[5]

Four days after arriving, Ryan, having visited Jonestown, was on his way home. He never made it. His entourage—along with twenty-six church members who had elected to leave the commune—were confronted by gunmen sent by Jones to the airstrip where two planes waited to take the group back to the United States.[6] What ensued was a hail of gunfire that killed Ryan, two newsmen, and a Temple defector, as well as seriously wounding five others.[7]

Simultaneous with that attack, Jones initiated a plan that involved the compulsory suicide of all members of the community. To that end, he had assistants pass around cups filled with grape Flavor Aid laced with a tranquilizer and cyanide. With the children, who could not be relied on to drink the poison willingly, Jones had aides inject the cyanide into their mouths via syringe. The adults who resisted were forcibly given the lethal beverage. Jones, messianic amid the madness he had set loose, continued to preach as people died around him. He proclaimed amid the carnage, "We committed an act of revolutionary suicide protesting the conditions of an inhumane world."[8]

These events in Guyana were shocking almost beyond comprehension. Making sense of the horror has led most popular representations to focus on the cult aspects of Jones and his Peoples Temple. Mostly lost in such accounts is the complexity of the church, which included a mix of spirituality, utopianism, antiracism, and socialism.[9]

In Jones's view, there was no distinction between socialism and the central tenets of Christianity. As he said, "If you're born in this church, this socialist revolution, you're not born in sin. If you're born in capitalist America, racist America, or fascist America, then you're born in sin. But if you're born in socialism, you're not born in sin."[10] Leaving aside the intellectual convolutions involved in coming to such an estimate, it was a result of such a radical ideology that the Peoples Temple attracted a diverse community, including a significant number of Black people, who felt alienated by and disgusted with the mainstream of U.S. society.

While it is understandable to a degree that Jones's political framework was not a major focus in the shock of the moment, it was nonetheless consequential. Among the reasons Jones had fled the Bay Area were his fear of coming repression in the United States and the appeal of Guyana's nominally socialist government led by its president Forbes Burnham.[11] In that respect, Jonestown, an idea realized amid the heightening of late Cold War contradictions, was hardly an outlier in its historical moment.

## Murder in City Hall

While San Francisco and the world were digesting events in Jonestown, Dan White—a former police officer, fireman, and Vietnam veteran—was in a state of murderous excitement.[12] The thirty-two-year-old White had until recently been a San Francisco supervisor—the equivalent of a city council member. He had been a conservative law-and-order advocate, but the position had not sat well with him. Citing financial reasons, he resigned from the post on November 10, 1978. He quickly, however, had a change of heart. As a result, he asked Mayor George Moscone to rescind the resignation. Unfortunately for White, however, the mayor had no interest in bringing him back. Moscone's failure to do so was seen by White as a betrayal.

That was what brought him to City Hall on the morning of November 27. His first stop was Moscone's office. As he entered, Moscone asked him, "What are you gonna do now, have you thought about it? You thinking about being a fireman again?"[13] White's response was to pull out a revolver and shoot the mayor twice in the head and twice in the abdomen, killing him.

He then made his way across the hall to the office of San Francisco supervisor Harvey Milk, whom he believed was sabotaging his reinstatement efforts. There, he challenged Milk, yelling, "What the hell are you doing to me? Why do you want to hurt my name, my family? You cheated me."[14] He then shot Milk twice in the back of the head and three times in his chest and stomach, killing him.[15]

White's emotional problems certainly ran deeper than disappointment with being denied a job he had left by his own decision—mentally healthy people do not go around killing people for such things. However, his actions had an impact beyond anything he was going through personally. That he had calculatingly murdered the city's first openly gay elected official set loose outrage among the city's gay population.

The evening after the killings, thirty thousand people gathered at city hall for a candlelight vigil. The new mayor, Dianne Feinstein, was on hand along with Joan Baez, who led the crowd in singing "Oh Freedom" and "Amazing Grace." The gathering also heard a tape of a speech by Milk, given three weeks earlier, where he proclaimed, "Every gay person should come out," to which the crowd responded with a wild cheer, holding their candles above their heads.[16]

Such expressions were but a foretaste of the resolve of the gay community to not go back to the oppressive status quo. This would become even clearer the following year with the fury unleashed in the wake of White's prosecution for murder.

## Foreshocks in Iran

While events in Guyana and San Francisco held the attention of a good section of the U.S. population, events in Iran, which had seen an escalating crisis in the previous years, were reaching a fever pitch.

When the country's Shah, Reza Pahlavi, visited the United States in November 1977, his appearance set off a tempest. Pro-Shah supporters confronted anti-regime protestors in Washington's Lafayette Park, prompting the police to fire teargas. Unfortunately for Jimmy Carter and the Shah, the direction of the wind that day sent the noxious gas wafting onto the White House lawn. The result was images going out across the wire of Carter and his wife Rosalynn wiping their eyes, having been gassed by their own police.[17]

The following year saw the situation deteriorate exponentially. Throughout November 1978 demonstrations in both the United States and Iran continued. In Tehran, the level of violence was boiling over. On November 1, twelve people were killed in clashes with the government. In the United States, Iranian students were routinely taking the streets to stand with their countrymen and women—including in Washington, DC, where twenty-five were arrested at an anti-Shah demonstration.[18]

Things would soon reach a point where *New York Times* columnist Hedrick Smith presented the assessment that matters were "completely out of control. . . . The Shah's present Government appears to be a lost cause for holding the line in this deteriorating situation."[19] Smith's assessment was portentous, as events would soon show.

## Guns on the Roof

Such simmering and actualized crises were impacting the musical and wider cultural scene. For most of 1978 popular music had been dominated by stultifying pop, mainstream rock, and omnipresent disco. As a counterpoint, punk rock, which had been incubating throughout 1974 and 1975, broke into the wider culture. In 1976 the Ramones released their eponymous album, which was followed by the Sex Pistols' *Never Mind the Bollocks* the next year. All of this was accompanied by a media barrage, which regardless of the particular takes, had the effect of popularizing the music to a far wider audience.

Nonetheless, this first wave of punk came and went relatively quickly. While the Ramones burned brightly throughout the seventies, 1976–1978 was arguably their most disruptive phase. The Sex Pistols, meanwhile, did not make it past 1978, disbanding at the end of their first and only U.S. tour.[20] Punk of course endured, engendering a host of bands—some more memorable than others. One of the most enduring, however, which arose at the same moment as the Ramones and the Sex Pistols, was just getting started in 1978.

The Clash formed the same year as the Sex Pistols. While they were known and had performed widely in the United Kingdom, their 1977 eponymous album, which did well in England, was not even released in America. CBS, their record company, claimed the album was not radio-friendly—though as an import it sold a hundred thousand copies.[21] With no U.S. release or radio exposure, it is little surprise that the group had not performed in the country. This would change in November 1978 with the release of their second album, *Give 'Em Enough Rope*. That record further articulated the group's pointed social criticism and rebellious energy.

While the punk movement as a whole embodied anger and alienation, what the Clash brought to the table was an ostensibly left-wing, if politically independent, sensibility. One need look no further than the cover art on *Give 'Em Enough Rope*. The album's jacket featured an image of vultures feeding on the corpse of a dead cowboy in the desert, with a Chinese Red Army soldier on horseback looking on. On the back jacket are a multitude of soldiers, three of whom hold large red flags.[22] The communist iconography was a deliberate statement. There was a trend among some in the punk scene to don fascist symbols for their shock value. For example, Siouxsie Sioux wore a swastika armband, and Sid Vicious had a leather jacket with a swastika on the back.[23] This trend was especially problematic as it played out at a time when Britain's virulently anti-immigrant National Front was gaining currency. In response to such things, Clash member Mick Jones had worn a Red Guard armband, making a counterstatement against such displays.[24]

Beyond the album cover, the album itself went deeper than most music of its time. In songs such as "Guns on the Roof," the group described a system built "by the sweat of the many," while "Tommy Gun" skewered terrorist political violence and "English Civil War"—an adaptation of "Johnny Comes Marching Home," a song written during the U.S. Civil War—captured the polarization in the United Kingdom in the mid-seventies. In the words of *Rolling Stone* critic Mikal Gilmore, the album surged "with visions of civil strife, gunplay, backbiting and lyrics that might've been spirited from the streets of Italy and Iran."[25] The album served as a sharp prequel for what the band would undertake the following year with a tour and album that memorialized key events of 1979.

There were other consequential, if less sensational, developments that November. The Soviet Union and Vietnam signed a "peace and friendship" treaty, solidifying their alliance; the United States and the United Kingdom conducted a joint nuclear test ninety miles northwest of Las Vegas, this after the Soviet Union carried out its own test in Western Siberia a few weeks earlier; and it was announced that Menachem Begin and Anwar Sadat were being put forward for the Nobel Peace Prize for their agreement that removed Egypt as a threat to Israel—and made it a huge benefactor of U.S. military aid.[26] As a whole, the flurry of events in November 1978 eluded fuller comprehension at the moment. In hindsight, however, they read as a prequel to the turmoil about to unfold as the calendar advanced into 1979.

# 2

# Marg bar Shah! (Death to the Shah!)

> Possibilities of blowback against the United States should always be in the back of the minds of all CIA officers involved in this type of operation.
>
> —DONALD WILBER, March 1954

Farzad was running late. On his way uptown to join fellow Iranian students, he confronted a typical 1970s-era New York subway dilemma. Standing on the downtown platform, he needed to be on the uptown side and had no way to get to the other side without exiting, crossing the street, and paying another fare. Rather than going through such costly and time-consuming maneuvers, he did the most expedient—if not necessarily the safest—thing. He jumped onto the tracks, gingerly navigating the electrified third rail, and ran to the opposite platform. In his haste, however, he caught his big toe on one of the tracks, breaking it. Nonetheless, he achieved his aim and arrived in Harlem where he joined his fellow students for a march and rally against the Shah. The Iranian students he joined had chosen to meet in Harlem out of solidarity with African American people in the United States. From that point, they set out on the eight-mile march down to Union Square in lower Manhattan.

As sacrifices go, undertaking an extensive march with a broken toe was a modest one—far bigger things were being extracted from people in Iran. It was, nonetheless, emblematic of a deeper commitment. The majority of Iranians, in the United States and in Iran, were not inclined to let anything stop them in their efforts to overthrow the Shah. That resolve would soon have world-shifting implications.[1]

## The Coup

In August 1953, the United States, unhappy with the Iranian prime minister's nationalizing of the oil industry and fearing the country might be lost to communism, worked with British and Iranian reactionaries to overthrow Mohammad Mosaddegh. As foreign interventions go, in the short term anyways, this was among the most successful the CIA had ever been involved in. The popularly elected government of a giant petroleum-rich nation, with a massive border with the Soviet Union, was removed. In its place a friendly pro-U.S. reactionary was installed, one who would ruthlessly rule the country for the next quarter century.[2]

The coup was the product of the mutual interests of discordant allies: the United States, the United Kingdom, and Iran's Ayatollah Abolqasem Kashani.[3] Plans for the coup were approved and funded at the highest level of the U.S. government.

Begun on August 15, 1953, the scheme initially wavered, when Mossadegh became aware of the plan and arrested the plotters. This in turn forced the Shah to flee the country for the safety of Greece. Things had gone so badly that on August 18, CIA headquarters ordered the operation to be halted. However, the CIA station chief in Iran, Kermit Roosevelt, ignored the order and redoubled efforts. With the aid of the Iranian military leadership of General Fazlollah Zahedi, the pro-Shah forces were then able to overwhelm security forces in the prime minister's compound, this after the troops and tanks supporting the coup squared off against the government's small arms fire.[4]

All of this was aided by the strategic support of Shiite cleric Ayatollah Kashani. Kashani, who had been an ally of Mossadegh in driving the British from Iran, had come to oppose the left turn of the government. As such, he called out his considerable supporters on August 19 to oppose Mossadegh.[5] As a result, the government fell, Mossadegh was arrested, and the Shah returned to Iran and assumed power.

The reaction in the United States was ecstatic. The Associated Press snidely reported, "Forces loyal to the absent Shah swept iron-willed weepy old Premier Mossadegh out of power today with a bloody and violent nine-hour coup." Notably, the ridicule revealed the ignorance of the role of public weeping in Iranian culture.[6] The *New York Times*, exhibiting a bit more restraint, nonetheless cast the manufactured coup as a popular uprising, reporting "Iranians loyal to Shah Mohammed Riza [*sic*] Pahlavi, including Tehran civilians, soldiers, and rural tribesmen, swept Premier Mohammed Mossadegh out of power today in a revolution."[7] It was a self-serving spin on what was essentially a foreign intervention.

Throughout this, the United States was adamant it had nothing to do with the coup. The day after, Brigadier General H. Norman Schwarzkopf—father of the 1991 Gulf War general—whom the press described as an "internationally recognized police expert," denied any role. When asked about meeting the Shah in Iran in early August, he dissembled, saying, "I went to pay my respects, that's all. I was passing through, and the Shah had asked me to call on him any time I was in the country."[8] That far-fetched explanation belied the fact that Schwarzkopf along with CIA Near-East station chief Kermit Roosevelt had worked in close consultation with the Shah to bring him back to power.[9] The result was a stunning accomplishment for the U.S. intelligence agency and the government it worked for. It was, however, an accomplishment the United States would come to pay a steep price for.

## Revolution in Iran

The Shah would go on to maintain power in Iran for the next twenty-six years. This was made possible in no small measure with the help of massive amounts of U.S. military and other aid, and the repressive efforts of the country's political police, SAVAK.[10] SAVAK was the product of assistance from the CIA, FBI, and the Israeli Mossad, which helped create the agency in 1957.[11] SAVAK would become notorious for hounding, jailing, and torturing anyone thought to be resisting the regime.[12] According to Frances Fitzgerald, niece of a former U.S. ambassador to Iran, SAVAK was omnipresent:

SAVAK has agents in the lobby of every hotel, in every government department, and in every university classroom. In the provinces, SAVAK runs a political intelligence-gathering service, and abroad it keeps a check on every Iranian student. . . . Educated Iranians cannot trust anyone beyond a close circle of friends, and for them, the effect is the same as if everyone else belonged. SAVAK intensifies this fear by giving no account of its activities. People disappear in Iran, and their disappearances go unrecorded. . . . The Shah says that his government has no political prisoners. (Communists, he explains, are not political offenders but common criminals.) Amnesty International estimates that there are about 20,000 of them.[13]

As formidable as SAVAK was, however, its days were numbered.

By the fall of 1978, the control of SAVAK and everything else about the Shah's rule, was coming apart. As one journalist described, "It's completely out of control. . . . The Shah's present Government appears to be a lost cause for holding the line in this deteriorating situation."[14] That situation included nationwide outrage after a fire at the Rex Theater in the southwestern Iranian city of Abadan—where the emergency doors were locked. The fire, which killed 370 people, was rumored to have been started by SAVAK, though the government claimed it was its opponents. Later investigations, however, suggested it was the work of Islamic extremists.[15] Regardless, the suspicions surrounding this horrific event were indicative of the loss of credibility of the regime.

Strikes and massive demonstrations were also at fever pitch. On September 8, after the Shah declared martial law, his army opened fire on demonstrators. Initial reports said hundreds, perhaps thousands, had been killed. While the actual number was likely closer to eighty, with a greater number of wounded, the viciousness of the action underscored the fact that for most Iranians that the Shah's regime was no longer tolerable. Things were moving toward a revolutionary resolution.[16]

By late November into December, the demonstrations continued and grew in size—a December 11 protest was modestly estimated as drawing a million people. According to historian Michael Axworthy, "The Shah lost the remainder of what in medieval Iran had been called *farr*—the aura of rightful kingship, associated with just rule and military success. People rejected him. They did not want to hear new suggestions or ideas from him, they just wanted him to go."[17] The days of the rule of the Shah were numbered. On December 31 it was announced that Shapur Bakhtiar would form a government and that the Shah was leaving the country to seek medical care. On January 16, 1979, he left Iran, never to return.[18]

What followed was a year of tumult with various secular and religious forces jockeying for power. In the end, it was the Shiite cleric Ayatollah Ruhollah Khomeini, who had been living in exile in France, who commanded the greatest following. He returned to the country on February 1 and on April 1 the Islamic Republic of Iran was declared. In the months following there was a contentious struggle, one in which those grouped around Khomeini maneuvered to capture the dominant power, including undermining and purging secular and leftist forces from the political scene.[19] Their effort would ultimately succeed.

## Shockwaves in the United States

Before 1978, demonstrating against the regime within Iran was a highly risky business. The Shah's secret police would routinely jail and torture dissidents in Tehran's notorious Evin Prison. Given that, a disproportionate responsibility for keeping alive the flames of opposition fell to Iranians living outside the country, especially students.[20] Not surprisingly then, when the level of discontent within Iran was reaching a crescendo, international protests rose in sync.

Throughout November and December 1978, demonstrators took to the streets of major U.S. cities. On November 1 in Washington, DC, twenty-four anti-Shah demonstrators were arrested in front of the White House after squaring off with U.S. Park Police.[21] The following month, more than two thousand Iranian students, who had gathered in San Francisco for their annual convention, blocked traffic outside the Iranian consulate and the federal building in protest against the Shah.[22] Two days later, hundreds of demonstrators in Beverly Hills clashed with police in a protest at the home of the Shah's sister, Princess Shams. To counter the demonstrators, police used tear gas and opened up fire hoses on the crowd. Thirty-two people were sent to the hospital.[23] It was the kind of turmoil more typical of the anti–Vietnam War demonstrations of the previous decade.

## The Iranian Students Association and the FBI

The Iranian Students Association (ISA) had a long history of protest within the United States and had been a potent ally of U.S. leftists. As a result, they were a target of the attention of not only their native SAVAK, but the FBI. A fact that is not surprising given the latter's role in creating that secret police agency.

While demonstrations against the Shah were particularly intense in the late 1970s, they had been going on for some time. As such, they were an ongoing concern of the FBI. Of particular concern was the potential for an attack on the Shah when he visited the country. This can be seen in the following letter written to Special Agents in Charge (SAC) by J. Edgar Hoover in 1962: "The Bureau has received information to the effect that dissident Iranian students in this country might possibly undertake an assassination attempt against the Shah during his visit. Moreover, the State Department has expressed concern as to the possible adverse effects of any large-scale demonstrations which might occur during the Shah's visit. All offices should be most alert for any information regarding anti-Shah demonstrations, possible threats to the Shah or his party, or other data of intelligence interest in connection with his visit."[24] The memo also outlines specific actions to be taken, including liaison with local police: "Any data concerning possible violence or demonstrations should be immediately disseminated to local police authorities as well as to appropriate State Department security representatives locally."[25] In this way, the FBI effectively served as an auxiliary of SAVAK.

Notably, U.S. intelligence agencies were also spying on the ISA via its ongoing surveillance of domestic Maoists. For example, the FBI—and CIA—kept a keen watch on Susan Heiligman Frank. Frank, also known as Sue Warren, was a supporter of Maoist China and had been in the Communist Party USA before joining the Progressive Labor Party. In the course of watching her, the FBI pursued her ties with the ISA: "NY T-1 [an FBI informant] advised on

January 25, 1967, that on that date the subject [Frank] was contacted by NASHIN HATEMI at which time they discussed a date that she was to speak to a group in which HATEMI was involved. The lecture was scheduled for 9:00 P.M. on the following Friday at 750 8th Avenue New York."[26] The FBI report goes on to note that "NY T-5 [another informant] advised on September 7, 1967, that NASHIN HATEMI was Vice-President of the Iranian Students Association." That same informant reported on Frank speaking to Iranian students about the Cultural Revolution in China: "NY T-5 advised on May 11, 1967 that the subject was scheduled to speak to the Iranian Students Association Chapter at Fairleigh Dickinson University in New Jersey in the near future concerning the Cultural Revolution in China."[27] All of this shows again that for politicized Iranian students studying in the United States, it was not only SAVAK they needed to be wary of.

Not surprisingly the attention on ISA continued as events in Iran approached crisis levels. In 1977, as the situation there was deteriorating, the FBI described the group: "The Iranian Students Association (ISA) in the United States is described in its own literature as a member of the World Confederation of Iranian Students (WCIS). Founded in 1958, WCIS is a student federation active in the United States, Europe, Turkey and the USSR. It is dedicated to the defense of Iranian 'political, prisoners' and opposed to the Government of the Shah of Iran. WCIS is governed by the communist concept of 'democratic centralism' and supports the National Front, an Iranian political party opposed to the Shah's government."[28]

The same report goes on to characterize one of the group's factions: "The (Marxist) Communist faction is opposed to armed struggle and guerrilla activity at the present stage. They cling to the orthodox Marxist view that the revolutionary consciousness of the peasants and workers must be raised before the revolution can succeed. They insist the only key to revolution is to follow the teachings of Marx, Lenin and MAO Tse-tung. They want to build alliances with revolutionary groups of other nations to present a broad united front against imperialism."[29] This was only one faction; the various political trends within the ISA, like those within Iran, were diverse. As the *Washington Post* noted, reporting on the makeup of a demonstration in 1977, opposition to the Shah ranged from "followers of the conservative Islamic Shiite sect to Marxists, socialists, and other unaligned leftists." As one of the demonstration's leaders said, "We have many ideologies, but we are united in overthrowing the shah."[30] That unity, tentative as it was, mirrored that in place in Iran.

What was notable in all this, however, was the sophistication on the part of the FBI in parsing out the politics of the various factions. That said, the unifying points that held Iranians together in both Iran and the United States were coming under increasing strain, as Khomeini and his followers pushed to consolidate their rule throughout 1979. All of which would soon come to a head as things lurched toward another crisis.

## Hostage Crisis

On October 23, 1979, the ailing Shah entered the United States for the treatment of cancer. From the standpoint of the United States, it was a courtesy extended to someone who had served their interests for so long. For Iranians, it was a high insult. They did not want the Shah to get world-class healthcare, they wanted him home where he could face trial. Beyond that, his entry into the United States—because of the CIA's earlier machinations—raised suspicions of an impending coup.

In response, on November 4, several hundred unarmed students broke into the U.S. embassy in Tehran. Inside they detained the sixty-three members of the diplomatic staff—including CIA agents deployed there—and the marines tasked with guarding the

Iran, 1979. Photo: Source unknown.

building.[31] While the marines brandished their weapons, there was no shooting—though there were some tear gas grenades fired. The mood of the students was mixed. One student who passed a nervous marine said, "Don't worry, you're safe. We won't hurt anyone." However, in other instances, several of the staff who had been taken hostage were beaten and threatened. This violence was particularly directed at those suspected of being with the CIA; it was also to coerce the hostages to open the embassy's safes.[32]

For the United States, this was a crisis with few good options. While Iranians may have feared a return of the Shah, the United States had been attempting to set up working relations with the emerging government. This can be seen in a confidential memo drawn up by Paul B. Heinze, a former CIA station chief in Turkey, for National Security Advisor Zbigniew Brzezinski. While Heinze admitted to not having any "original thoughts" on how to get the hostages released, he did have ideas on the strategic implications of what was underway. As he wrote, the United States needed to "think beyond the current imbroglio and not let emotions generated during it undermine our longer-term interests

in this part of the world." In that respect, his main concern was
what this meant regarding the Soviets:

> If there is leftist and/or Soviet input, directly or indirectly, into the
> Embassy takeover, the aim can only be to make it impossible for us
> to have any relations with Iran over an extended period of time. The
> fact that we were on the way to re-establishing a military relation-
> ship and American business was still able to function was inimical
> to leftist objectives. It is in the long-term interest of the left, much
> more than that of the religious fanatics, to have us out of Iran
> entirely; but it is very convenient for the left (whether they are
> manipulating or influencing the situation or not) to have the
> religious fanatics doing their work for them.[33]

A couple of things stand out here. First is the memo's underestima-
tion of how problematic the rule of the mullahs was going to be
for the United States. Beyond that, it is clear that the particular fate
of the hostages was of less concern than the United States' overall
position vis-à-vis its contention with the Soviet Union.

This did not mean that the government and media were not
feverishly whipping up anti-Iranian sentiment around the hostages.
The editorial page of the *Washington Post*, while cautioning that
the United States "should not act in a way likely to endanger the
Americans being held hostage," it should also not display "pussy-
cat acquiescence in the reckless way the Iranian authorities-cum-
mob are behaving." One suggestion offered was for the government
to "find ways to return some of those visiting and protesting
Iranians in this country if they have violated the terms of their
stay."[34] In other words speedy deportations—especially for student
activists.

That call would soon turn into a national targeting, one with a
sharp xenophobic edge. For example, in Houston, five hundred
"Texans" surrounded the main entrance of the Iranian consulate
to demand the release of the hostages. The mob chanted "Iranians
go home!" while waving signs reading "Keep the Shah and Send

Them Carter," "Death to Khomeini," and "Camel Jockeys Go Home."[35] Meantime, in Philadelphia, fifty construction workers marched to city hall in protest of Iranian student demonstrations. On the West Coast, at Fresno State University, demonstrators waved signs reading "Have a Happy Thanksgiving—Hold an Iranian Hostage," "Deport Iranians," and "Send in the Marines."[36] A similar tone was set in Springfield, Massachusetts, where a small group of city employees burned an Iranian flag on the steps of city hall. Even more volatilely, Iranian students were physically attacked on the campus of Pittsburg State University by a man wearing a ski mask.[37] That these events were duly recorded in the media was not simply "keeping the public informed," but served as a kind of popularization.

Along with this, authorities moved to stop protests by Iranians. In Los Angeles officials banned a Beverly Hills march planned by Iranian students. Similarly, in Washington, DC, Mayor Marion Barry was jeered after allowing Iranian students to proceed with a permitted march. In response, he canceled permits for a protest the following day.[38] All of this was setting a tone. An entire generation of youth in America were being indoctrinated in how to view the people of "I-Ran" as a mob of "camel jockeys" and "hadjis" deserving of being bombed into oblivion. It was an ominous undertaking that bode bad things to come, not just for people in Iran but for the majority of people living in the Middle East.

These events also held long-term negative consequences for the United States. In the wake of the 1953 coup in Iran, the CIA set down an "after-action report" in which the agency introduced the term "blowback" into the lexicon.[39] The word was used to denote the unintended fallout of covert actions. Events in Iran during 1978 and 1979 were a living example of what that meant. Unfortunately for the United States, there would soon be another crisis to be confronted, one involving literal fallout.

# 3

# From Harrisburg
# to Sverdlovsk

I don't know whether to cry my
eyes out, scream my head off,
or wet my pants.

**—POSTER OF A DISTRESSED INFANT**,
hanging in the Three Mile Island
Control Room

At 4 A.M. on March 28, 1979, the Three Mile Island (TMI) nuclear
power plant in Middletown, Pennsylvania, twenty minutes down
the Susquehanna River from the state capitol in Harrisburg, lurched
into crisis. Unbeknown to the technicians manning the control
room, after a minor heat rise had caused the reactor to shut down,
a valve that should have closed remained open. When the reactor
restarted, coolant water meant to keep the core of the nuclear reactor stable instead drained away.[1]

What followed were days of high tension, with those responsible for the power plant attempting to get ahead of a crisis none of them thought would ever happen. Undergirding events was the simple fact that TMI was a commercial enterprise, operating according to the dictates of business. The first public response of Metropolitan Edison, the power company that operated the plant, was minimization. Blaine Fabian, a spokesman for the company reassuringly told the press that "this is not a 'China Syndrome' type situation." This was a reference to a film that had just been released whose title was industry slang for a catastrophic meltdown, where an uncooled nuclear reactor core burned hundreds of feet into the earth—that is, all the way to China.[2]

For its part, the government was dealing with bad and conflicting information. Regardless, it put a premium on projecting calm—despite the dangerous uncertainty. Pennsylvania state authorities did not immediately order an evacuation—which was logically merited. Later, as the situation degenerated, after first having advised people to "stay inside," they shifted to suggesting pregnant women leave the area. Such equivocation only worsened matters and eroded their credibility.[3]

Throughout the crisis loomed the possibility of a meltdown—a situation that could have led to the release of massive amounts of highly toxic radioactive material.[4] While a radiation release does not carry the dramatic flourish of a nuclear weapon's mushroom cloud and fireball, it is no less a horrible prospect, and can mean death on a mass scale. A release of radioactive material is a deceptively quiet matter, invisible to the human eye. Lacking the proper testing material, people would likely not know they had been exposed until symptoms started appearing. However, if people were subject to a high enough dose they would immediately succumb to vomiting, diarrhea, headache, fever, dizziness, disorientation, weakness, and fatigue. Complicating matters, a first round of sickness might abate, only to be followed by renewed and unrelenting symptoms. In cases where exposure is beyond a certain point—anywhere from four hundred to five hundred rems of radiation in

Cleanup crew at Three Mile Island, March 1979. Photo: *Report of The Presidents Commission on the Accident at Three Mile Island.*

a short period—the most likely outcome of the exposure is death.[5] In other words, radiation at meltdown levels is a massively lethal event for those exposed to it.

## The China Syndrome

The accident at TMI occurred at a time when the United States— because of the Organization of the Arab Petroleum Exporting Countries (OAPEC) oil embargo—confronted the need for alternate sources of energy. As such, nuclear power had a good deal of support from the powers that be, including President Carter, a nuclear energy advocate who had worked aboard a nuclear-powered submarine when he was in the U.S. Navy. Given that, the arrival of a film portraying the dangers of nuclear power in 1979 was not a welcome event.

*The China Syndrome*, released on March 16, was a fictional account of a nuclear accident. Set in California, the film's lead character, portrayed by Jack Lemmon, becomes concerned after a safety scare at the plant. This leads him to discover that the contractor who built the plant had cut corners, creating a dangerous situation. Meantime, the characters played by Jane Fonda and Michael Douglas—a newswoman and cameraman—who had witnessed the scare, set out to expose the larger danger. Beyond employing filmmaking essentials that turned this into a melodrama with a tragic, but ultimately safe ending, the film introduced the wider public to certain realities about nuclear power.

In contrast to the film's oppositional narrative, however, there was powerful support for nuclear energy among key elements of the country's ruling forces and opinion makers. This could be seen, for example, via journalist George Will. Will, intent on challenging the film's liberal pretensions, breezily asserted in a column that there "is more cancer risk in sitting next to a smoker than next to a nuclear power plant."[6] It was a fallacious argument that would be shown false almost at the moment it was made.

In some respects, the accident at TMI was more insidious than the scenario that played out in *The China Syndrome*. While the movie dealt with the corruption of a contractor trying to save money by forging the X-rays of welds rather than properly inspecting them, TMI appears to have not involved brazen malfeasance. Instead, it was a matter of humans refusing to believe they had built something they might not be able to control.

As later studies of the event documented, the experts at the Metropolitan Edison power company and the Nuclear Regulatory Commission consistently misapprehended the depth of the crisis.

Things were such that people manning the control center chose to believe their gauges were giving them more alarming readings than were actually in existence. Compounding such denial was the fact that one inspector, James Creswell, had discovered the flaw with the faulty valve, the same type that affected TMI, in 1977 at an Ohio plant. That flaw also existed in nine other nuclear plants. However, bureaucratic resistance kept that information from being acted on—including in a meeting held six days before the TMI event.[7]

The crisis at TMI was a perfect storm. It was an accident that baffled those responsible for bringing it under control, at a moment when a popular film had alerted a large audience to what a worst-case scenario of a nuclear accident would be, and one in which the relevant authorities blundered and blundered again in communicating the situation in an effort to pacify the public. While in the end the reactor was able to be brought under control, and the consequences were not as dire as some had predicted, the whole notion of an energy source ultimately outside the power of humans to control—and with the potential for inflicting death on a large scale—was put forward front and center in the public's consciousness.

## No Nukes

TMI came at a time when a good amount of residual sixties activism had been channeled into environmental issues, especially those dealing with nuclear power. This included opposing power plants such as the ones in Diablo Canyon in California, Hanford in Washington State, and Indian Point in New York. These movements in turn attracted the support of prominent artists such as Jackson Browne, Graham Nash, and Bonnie Raitt, all of whom would become board members of an organization called Musicians United for Safe Energy (MUSE). On the heels of the near-disaster in

Pennsylvania, that group organized a series of five concerts, four in Madison Square Garden and one outdoors in New York's Battery Park. They were branded the "MUSE Concerts for a Non-Nuclear Future" and aimed at raising money for the anti-nuclear cause.

Scheduled in September, the shows highlighted veteran artists such as Crosby, Stills & Nash, James Taylor, Carly Simon, and Jesse Colin Young, but also seventies rock stars such as Tom Petty and the Heartbreakers, the Doobie Brothers, and Bruce Springsteen & the East Street Band. Also performing were singer John Hall—an organizer of the event and later a congressman—Peter Tosh, Ry Coder, Chaka Khan, Sweet Honey in the Rock, Poco, and Gil Scott-Heron. Scott-Heron, the most highly charged political artist, performed his song "We Almost Lost Detroit" about a nuclear accident to the south of that city at Madison Square Garden, but it was only at the outdoor concert that he showcased his highly political songs: "Johannesburg," "Winter in America," and "The Revolution Will Not Be Televised." None of those made their way onto the concert album.

There was hope going into the concerts that they would spearhead renewed activism. As one profile noted, "The MUSE concerts are already being hailed in some quarters as 'the end of the "me" decade' of the 1970's—a decade often characterized by self-absorption at the expense of social concern and political involvement."[8] That type of description was a recurring theme of the time. The sixties were not so far in the past in 1979, and, as such, they were used as a ready gauge for what might be expected from political activism. The fact that things were instead headed in an altogether different direction was not so apparent.

The changed times explain why the MUSE concerts did not register in the way such events as the Monterey Pop Festival or Woodstock did. The problem was not so much the artists, but something more intangible. The Doobie Brothers may have sung "Takin' It to the Streets," but it served more as a good-time concert moment than an actual call to arms.[9] As the *New York Times*' John Rockwell—who generally gave the show good marks—assessed, "On the whole, the experience was numbing; five and a half hours of music is too much, especially when most of it is confined to a fairly narrow stylistic range."[10]

One notable exception was Bruce Springsteen—who seemed more keyed into the unfolding moment.[11] His most riveting song in that regard was "The River," about a young man who marries a young woman he had gotten pregnant when "she was just seventeen." It is a song set against a backdrop of a fraying economy, diminished expectations, and broken dreams. Springsteen would have much more to say about such things in the immediate years to follow.

## The End of Détente

Nuclear energy may have been the nominal concern motivating certain activists at the end of the seventies, but there was something else looming that conjured up images more horrific than a meltdown: a potential world war and the nuclear weapons that would be employed to fight it.

Since the Cuban Missile Crisis of 1962, when the Soviet Union and the United States squared off over the former's deploying of nuclear weapons in Cuba—bringing the world the closest it had ever come to a bilateral nuclear exchange—the matter of nuclear war had been to a degree put into the background. However, with the rapprochement between the United States and China and the corresponding shift in the geopolitical balance of power, nuclear contention between the United States and the Soviet Union came vaulting back to life. This was the situation going into the second round of negotiations between the United States and the Soviet Union, known as the Strategic Arms Limitations Talks (SALT). These negotiations took place in the period of détente, or easing of tensions, between the two superpowers.

The first SALT agreement had been hammered out while Nixon was president. That treaty put limits on certain nuclear missiles, specifically the anti-ballistic missile sites being built to counter incoming nukes, and the offensive intercontinental ballistic missiles (ICBMs).[12] The limit on ICBMs was of strategic importance given those weapons are able to travel up to six thousand miles—the approximate distance between Washington, DC, and Moscow. A single ICBM could deliver a nuclear warhead equivalent to a hundred kilotons of dynamite, which if dropped on New York could kill over a half million people.[13] The treaty also set limits on how many other offensive missiles each country could retain.[14]

While the treaty signaled a reluctance to engage in nuclear brinkmanship, it was not primarily at reducing the superpowers' existing arsenals, which were large enough to destroy a good deal, if not all, of humanity. Rather, it was focused on checking the expansion of certain types of weapons.

Nixon and Soviet premier Leonid Brezhnev met in Moscow to sign SALT I in 1972. Following that were negotiations leading to what would be called the Vladivostok Agreement, signed in 1974 by then president Gerald Ford and Brezhnev. This modified the initial treaty to make the United States and Soviets able to have "only" 2,400 land-based and submarine-based missiles each.[15]

This formed the backdrop to the SALT II treaty, which aimed at further reducing the number of missiles.[16] While that agreement was completed and executed by both Jimmy Carter and Brezhnev—who embraced after its signing—it immediately ran into trouble in Congress. Howard Baker, who at the time was the Senate minority leader, called the agreement "fatally flawed." By his account, it allowed the Soviets to retain a class of missiles—the so-called blockbusters—that the United States had no equivalent for. Such opposition in turn led to calls to renegotiate, an idea Soviet foreign minister Andrei Gromyko firmly opposed.[17] Because of this, the agreement stalled. SALT II was essentially DOA.[18]

## New Weapons and Agencies

The SALT talks were about weapons already in existence, but both the Soviet Union and the United States were feverishly at work producing new and more deadly instruments. This included nuclear and, for the Soviets, biological weapons.

In the United States, there was a good deal of effort put into producing something called an "enhanced radiation weapon," which would become known as the neutron bomb. The project was secret until word of the weapon's development was leaked in June 1977 after journalist Walter Pincus discovered its details buried in a congressional budget report.[19] Unlike conventional nuclear weapons, the neutron bomb was designed to emit a huge dose of lethal radiation, which could penetrate military hardware, like tanks, without emitting the blast of conventional nukes. As such, it was seen as a tactical weapon that would benefit the warfighting capacity of North Atlantic Treaty Organization (NATO) forces against the Soviets. However, when word of the weapon became public it created huge pushback. As a result, President Carter was forced to shelve its imminent development. Regardless, the project was not abandoned entirely. The neutron bomb did go into production, though it was not deployed—at least as is publicly known.[20] In a similar fashion, Carter also greenlit the MX missile, an intercontinental weapon that contained 1,012 warheads that could be aimed at individual targets.[21] Unlike the neutron bomb, the MX was deployed, though not until Carter had left office.

Along with such weapons development came Executive Order 12148, which called for the consolidation of a number of federal emergency response agencies into a single entity, the Federal Emergency Management Agency (FEMA).[22] While one aspect of FEMA's mandate was to respond to incidents like the partial meltdown at TMI, there was another. FEMA would be responsible for preparing the country for nuclear war, or as the government outlined, for "the protection of the Nation's population from nuclear weapons' effects." This included responsibility for undertaking "studies of population relocation to areas less vulnerable to attack" and "the protection of critical industries from destruction in case of enemy attack."[23] TMI might have pointed up the need for a certain type of emergency plans, but being prepared for a nuclear attack on the United States was also now being given serious attention.


## Biological Weapons

Amid much fanfare, in November 1969 Richard Nixon declared the United States was renouncing the use of biological weapons. This included the deadly pathogen anthrax, brucellosis, and Staphylococcal enterotoxin B. As a result of Nixon's move, the United States' stockpile of such weapons would be destroyed.[24] Along with those agents, the measure included most of the country's chemical weapons, with the exception of defoliants and tear gas—still in abundant use in Vietnam (and on the nation's campuses).[25]

On the whole, what was given up was not critical in warfighting, but bioweapons were considered especially problematic. As critics of their use pointed out there was no guarantee weaponized pathogens could be "kept from spreading into neutral or friendly territories or even from triggering a worldwide 'pandemic' that would boomerang on the United States."[26] Unlike nuclear missiles, which could be dispatched with a certain precision, bioweapons were freighted with the possibility of devastating blowback. But there was an even bigger calculation in why Nixon did not feel wedded to such weapons. The truth of this comes by way of an offhand remark by Nixon to his then speechwriter William Safire. As Safire recalled: "I've been interested in the lingo of bio-war ever since 1970, when President Nixon told me, one of his speech writers, to draft a renunciation of U.S. use of biological weapons and to announce the destruction of our stockpile. Shouldn't we keep a few, I asked, in case we needed to retaliate someday? 'We'll never use the damn germs,' he replied, 'so what good is biological warfare as a deterrent? If somebody uses germs on us, we'll nuke 'em.'"[27] Nixon's announcement initiated a process that would be completed in 1975, at which point Gerald Ford was president. It was then that the United Kingdom joined the Soviet Union and the United States in renouncing biological weapons.[28] There was a problem, however. The Soviet Union never actually stopped producing them.

## Anthrax in the Urals

Four days after radioactive material escaped from the TMI nuclear plant, a different type of poison was wafting through the air in the city of Sverdlovsk (now called Yekaterinburg), east of the Ural Mountains in the Soviet Union. Sometime between 6 A.M. and 8 A.M. on April 2, 1979, a deadly burst of weaponized anthrax—in the form of airborne spores—shot into the air outside the secret military site called Compound-19, on the southern edge of the city. How the spores escaped the facility is still unknown; one theory holds a protective filter had been removed and was not properly replaced. Regardless of the cause, the results were immediate.[29]

Under normal conditions, anthrax is a bacterial disease that mainly afflicts sheep and cattle. However, in the early twentieth century, researchers discovered that lethal bacteria could be weaponized for use against humans, by turning it into a powder that could be sent floating through the air, infecting anyone unlucky enough to breathe it in. While the symptoms of inhaling anthrax—headache, coughing, mild fever, chills, and grogginess—take a day or two to emerge, they quickly escalate, eventually overpowering the immune system and leading to death.[30]

Weaponized anthrax was first used during World War I. In one instance, Germany deliberately infected Argentinian livestock, with plans—never carried out—to poison the Allied powers' food supply. It was also used by the Japanese when they invaded

Manchuria in 1932—with some projections indicating they infected (and killed) upward of ten thousand people.[31] On the heels of that, during World War II both the United States and the United Kingdom began aggressive experimentation with anthrax. While it was never deployed, the United States did fill five thousand bombs with the germ in preparation for a possible attack by Germany. After the war, the United States actively tested biological weapons. In one experiment, dubbed "Operation Sea-Spray," the military tested the efficacy of weaponized bio agents by using giant hoses to spray a bacteria cloud of *Serratia marcescens* and *Bacillus globigii* from a U.S. Navy ship docked off the coast of San Francisco. At the time *S. marcescens* was thought to be benign, though it was later learned that it can cause infections of the urinary and respiratory tract. In the San Francisco test, at least one person died and ten others were hospitalized—it is unclear exactly how many were impacted.[32]

In Sverdlovsk, this was not a test with nominally benign bacteria. Rather, the bacteria were deliberately weaponized for lethality. Given that, the accidental release resulted in at least sixty fatalities—though the exact number is again unclear.[33] At the time, the Soviets, attempting to cover up the release, claimed the illnesses were a result of "contaminated meat."[34] Not only were they keen to cover up the incident for sickening its own population, but they were officially bound by a treaty banning the use of the weapons they were creating.

It was, however, too catastrophic to keep secret long. According to Tom Mangold and Jeff Goldberg in their book *Plague Wars*, "Most of the first casualties were located within a few hundred yards downwind of the anthrax plant. They included people who just happened to be near open windows, standing outside, or walking in the street. The worst affected were military personnel from the production site, troops stationed at the adjacent Compound 32, various men on their way to work, and about twenty people already working at a nearby ceramics factory."[35] All this was compounded by the secrecy in place. The civilian doctors, who had never encountered the effects of weaponized anthrax, were unaware there was a secret military production site in town. As such, they had no way of knowing, at least in the first few days, what they were confronting.[36]

Any one of the manifold crises and undertakings that occurred in 1979—the accident at TMI, the anthrax leak in Sverdlovsk, or the production of even more deadly nuclear weapons—would have been enough to call into question the relative passivity that had been in place in the middle years of the seventies. Taken in aggregate, they signaled the United States and the world had crossed over onto new and more dangerous ground.

# 4

# Economic
# Dislocations

The standard of living of the average
American has to decline.

**—CHAIRMAN OF THE FEDERAL
RESERVE PAUL VOLKER,**
October 1979

On February 19, 1960, Samuel D. Earl, president of Standard Furniture of Herkimer, New York, a maker of high-quality wooden
desks, shot and killed himself. Earl's company had been under
financial pressure, not the least from aluminum and metal desk
makers who were grabbing a bigger share of the market. In the
weeks before his suicide, the government had slapped him with a
lien for unpaid withholding taxes. Meantime, a scheme to raise
money from local residents—which yielded $200,000—failed to
allay the problems. At the time of his suicide, he was confronting
not being able to meet the latest payroll. His death, however, solved

his financial, if not his personal, problems. Specifically, it triggered an insurance payout of $700,000 (about $7 million today) that guaranteed the company's "continued operations in the event of his death." That was sufficient to allow the business to carry on, which it did.

In 1979, however, there was nothing, not even the desperate actions of a factory owner, that could save Standard Furniture, a company in operation since 1886.[1] The factory unceremoniously closed, never to return. While the incident was a major event for Herkimer, it registered no mention in the national media. Compared to the avalanche of bad economic news coursing through the country—from the closings of major steel mills, the juggernaut of automation, and the adoption of a philosophy hostile to working people—the Standard Furniture story did not even merit a footnote. It was but a cellular disturbance amid a major organic shift.

## Gold, Oil, and Crisis

President Richard Nixon took to television in August 1971 to announce the United States would no longer redeem foreign currency for a fixed amount of gold—instead, the dollar would float on the open market to determine its value.[2] The move was taken to address a matter of increasing worry by the leaders of the United States. As the State Department described things, "By the 1960s, a surplus of U.S. dollars caused by foreign aid, military spending, and foreign investment threatened this system, as the United States did not have enough gold to cover the volume of dollars in worldwide circulation at the rate of $35 per ounce; as a result, the dollar was overvalued."[3]

In defending the move Nixon said, "We must create more and better jobs; we must stop the rise in the cost of living; we must protect the dollar from the attacks of international money speculators." In the short term, it seemed to work. Shortly after the plan was implemented, employment and production in the United States did increase. Inflation too was practically halted during a ninety-day wage-price freeze Nixon had implemented.[4] However, inflation—and worse—would soon return. The underlying problem was that the U.S. dollar—which had funded the war in Vietnam and kept the country economically stable—no longer held its previous value. Unfortunately, Nixon would soon have another problem.

In October 1973 Israel went to war with Egypt and Syria, who were attempting to retake territory Israel had occupied since its six-day war of 1967. In response, the United States came to Israel's assistance. Nixon went to Congress and asked for $2.2 billion (about $14 billion today) in aid.[5] That support prompted OAPEC to institute an oil embargo on the United States. That embargo stopped U.S. imports from key oil-producing countries such as Saudi Arabia, Iraq, and Kuwait. Those countries also began a series of production cuts that drove up the price of this essential commodity. By January 1974, the price of a barrel of oil had quadrupled. An energy crisis followed in which the price of gas in the United States skyrocketed while its availability plummeted.

The United States, a country predicated on everyone having an automobile, suddenly found itself "out of gas." As the *Washington Post* opined, "If Vietnam and Watergate taught Americans to mistrust their leaders, the energy crisis taught them that government didn't work."[6] It was an unprecedented blow to the unspoken assumptions about what life in the United States was supposed to be about.

## Economic Shifts

All this was playing out amid tectonic economic changes. While small towns such as the one described above were one indicator of change, they were only a small part. More consequential were the industrial powerhouse cities such as Philadelphia, Baltimore, and Chicago—which were in the midst of losing over a third of their manufacturing jobs.[7]

On the surface, the United States was still a global manufacturing leader. It was not until June 1979 that the country hit its peak for the number of workers employed in industry. However—looked at on a per capita basis—the peak had already been reached.[8] And while the flight of industry to China lay in the future, moves to the U.S. South—and its business-friendly anti-union environment—were well underway.[9]

Beyond that, were relocations overseas. Countries such as South Korea, Taiwan, Singapore, Hong Kong, Brazil, and Mexico were attracting more and more industry. In the seventies, those countries exhibited a significant economic growth rate of 7.5 percent. Along with this was an increase in the number of goods manufactured in these countries, which came to an average of more than 13 percent per year. By 1979 they were supplying the West with nearly 40 percent of its clothing imports. Even Japan and Germany were involved, staking a claim in the market for auto manufacturing, with Japan also stepping up production in consumer electronics.[10] The consequence of all this was an expansion of the manufacturing economy in some parts of the world—knitting it into a globalized fabric—and a corresponding shrinkage in the United States.

This was on stark display in some of the country's most populous urban cores. Philadelphia, once the nation's third-largest city, saw industry go from 27 percent of the city's employment base in 1970 to 17 percent a decade later.[11] Things were even starker in New York, where, in 1947, 1,047,030 people worked in manufacturing. By 1980 that number had been cut to 499,000.[12] What followed were fiscal crises, reduced services, and escalating rates of crime.[13] The consequences to the vibrancy, quality of life, and increased polarization in these urban behemoths cannot be overstated.

Things were such that the government held hearings to investigate—though a meaningful remedy was not forthcoming. In January 1979, a U.S. Senate committee was convened to look into plant closings in New Jersey. The hearings, held in Newark, were a forum for politicians and union representatives to speak about what was going on. One witness's description of a "runaway shop" is revealing of a process that had been in play for years, but which was hitting new milestones.

> THE CHAIRMAN [NJ SEN. HARRISON A. WILLIAMS JR.] Which one are you referring to?
>
> MR. [ARTHUR] COLE [INTERNATIONAL UNION OF ELECTRICAL WORKERS (IUE)] Westinghouse, Newark.
>
> MR. [JAKE] KONOWICH [IUE] Mr. Chairman, this is my second experience of a runaway. Approximately 20 years ago Westinghouse Corp. in Newark ran down to Raleigh, N.C., with 1,800 jobs. At that time our bread and butter product was the house meter. This was the baby making money for them. They left, and 1,800 people were laid off. We got down to approximately 400 or 500 people at that time. Since then, we have built up slightly, we went up to about 1,600 people. Then we started to backtrack again. Lo and behold, approximately 2 years ago we were called in, my committee was called in with the company, and we were informed that the company was thinking of either eliminating some products, moving partially, or moving completely.[14]

The witness then described how a Westinghouse plant in Metuchen, which had once employed 2,500, now made air conditioners with only five hundred workers.[15] The changes described here were incremental but cumulative—akin to boiling a frog in a pot, where the increasing heat is tolerable until it is lethal. A similar but more accelerated type of lethality was on display with U.S. Steel.

## The Problem of U.S. Steel

U.S. Steel was the largest steel maker in the United States. It was an institution and bedrock on which thousands had realized the American Dream. In 1979, that dream would take a major hit when in November the company announced it was closing three dozen of its plants and eliminating the jobs of more than thirteen thousand of its total workforce of 165,000. In making the announcement the company left open the possibility of further closings.[16]

There were myriad reasons for U.S. Steel's economic woes: the cost of labor was too high, environmental regulations too stringent, and foreign imports were cutting into profitability. All of these held true, but the biggest problem was that this U.S. industry had failed to modernize. In 1979, a modern Japanese steel factory—which had to import all the raw materials to make steel—could nonetheless make the product in forty-five minutes. By contrast, the U.S. Steel plant in Youngstown, Ohio, required eight hours to produce the same amount.[17] The effect on the bottom line was substantial. The *Washington Post*, citing a government economist, noted: "It costs Bethlehem Steel as much as 40 percent more per ton to make steel at Lackawanna [New York] than at Burns Harbor [the modern plant in Cleveland, Ohio]."[18] From a profit and loss perspective, this was an intolerable situation.

Youngstown, Ohio, was especially hard hit. According to one report, "The U.S. Steel closures, and more in the pipeline at Jones and Laughlin, and Republic Steel, would bring the number of lost jobs in the Youngstown steel industry in the last two years to more than 10,000." The effect on the Mahoning Valley area where Youngstown was located was devastating. The area would lose an estimated 75 percent of its income.[19] The city's lifeblood was being drained away.

What was taking place was not simply the loss of jobs, but the shredding of the social contract that had been in place for the American working class. This comes through in a report by a journalist visiting Ohio's U.S. Steel Workers' Local Union 1307. He begins his report by noting the presence of Cadillacs, then a prestige car, in the parking lot. He then writes, "Officials acknowledge the steel industry has built them a lifestyle it would be difficult to emulate in blue-collar work elsewhere . . . a detached house, children at college, and long hunting and fishing holidays in the spectacular Appalachian countryside." As the report continues, what becomes clear is that the disappearing jobs in the steel plants would mean the loss of all that.[20]

A similar crisis played out in Los Angeles at U.S. Steel's Torrance works. A profile in the *LA Times* of the closing described the jolting reality: "If you can look into a furnace at 3,000 degrees and handle liquid steel just like handling water, that's a skilled job. You've got to have strength and persistence to handle that type of work. Inside the factory, they're highly trained and highly paid. But when they hit the gates, they're just paid labor."[21] To which could be added, the amount that labor was going to be paid working in less lucrative industries would be a good deal less.

The same *LA Times* piece quoted a union official asking rhetorically, "Where is our electronics industry? It's gone. Where is our textile industry? It's gone. You and I are wearing shirts and coats made in Korea. And everyday factories are closing. . . . Sooner or later we will hit the bottom."[22] Similarly, an account in the UK *Guardian* pointed out, "As a result of the latest lay-offs across the industry, the foothold gained by the exporters could become a rush. Analysts say it could reach up to 50 percent by the mid-1980s— implying that huge areas of the US's industrial northeast might become waste lands."[23] That forecast would be far more prescient than the writer might have assumed.

## Automation

A big part of the problem for U.S. Steel was its failure to modernize its equipment and its focus on chasing profits through other schemes. As Staughton Lynd writes: "In 1979, the same year in which the shutdowns of the Youngstown Works and other steel facilities were announced, the company opened a new joint-venture shopping center near Pittsburgh containing the largest enclosed mall in Pennsylvania and, a few weeks after the Youngstown shutdown announcement, signed a letter of intent with Tenneco Chemicals, Inc. to build world-scale chemical facilities in

Houston."[24] Despite such side projects, the ability to produce the same commodity using less labor and resources was something they could not compete against. What U.S. Steel was not doing was retooling its plants to bring them in sync with late twentieth-century production standards.

Throughout this period an increasing number of manufacturing processes were being streamlined through automation. This was through refining mechanical procedures and increasingly utilizing computer technology. The woes of U.S. Steel were not unique; from steel to coal mining to telecommunications, formerly labor-intensive industries were being "revolutionized," to the detriment of the people who once made a living doing them.

As early as 1960, ten thousand jobs in steel production had already been lost to automation. Similarly, coal mining was being transformed. For example, in 1950 there were 125,000 pick-and-shovel miners working in West Virginia. That same year, coal operators began replacing these workers with digging machines. The result would lead to the loss of approximately seventy thousand mining jobs.[25] Also, in the 1970s coal companies introduced long-wall machines that extracted huge slabs of the earth to lay hold to the coal embedded in it. Then there was surface mining, where machines and explosions ripped the tops off mountains to seize the coal below, eliminating the need for even more coal miners.[26] The results were profound. In 1920, approximately 785,000 people worked in mining. By 1980, the number had shrunk to 242,000.[27]

Meantime, with more sophisticated technology, jobs beyond manufacturing simply disappeared. Once an essential element in printing, the Linotype operator gave way to the computer typesetter—a field that would also become extinct as computer technology advanced. Similarly, the seventies saw the introduction of the word processor, which would eliminate the position of the typist. That, too, would soon find itself replaced by more efficient computers. All of this transferred once-skilled work onto an array of professionals, from doctors to lawyers, to financial advisors. Their assistants, if they had one, would now be tasked with supporting multiple bosses. And in telecommunications, the number of operators—one of the few technology-based jobs available to women—dwindled as more and more sophisticated technology for relaying calls and managing phone networks was implemented.[28] It was a process that would only gain speed as time moved on, affecting one-time-stable employment prospects.

Between the flight of industry and the disruption automation brought, the country's economy was undergoing a transformation. It was one that disregarded the millions of people whose lives had centered on those disappearing jobs. While 1979 may have been the zenith of manufacturing employment, a look under the hood of what was happening revealed frightening developments for a critical section of the U.S. population.

## Neoliberalism

In sync with deindustrialization and automation came a political philosophy that conveniently acquitted the government of playing a role in aiding the people it nominally was empowered to protect.

In May 1979 Margaret Thatcher was elected prime minister of the United Kingdom. A good deal of media coverage at the time focused on her being the first woman prime minister and prognosticating on what that would mean. It was an interesting, and not wholly irrelevant, aspect, but it belied something more important about Thatcher's ascent. This is something Thatcher herself made clear in dismissing any notion of her bearing a feminist mantle: "I don't like strident females. I like people with ability who don't run the feminist wicket too hard. If you get somewhere it is because of your ability as a person not because of your sex."[29]

That dubious outlook taken into account, what was considerably more significant about Thatcher than her gender was her advocacy of a form of capitalism that was unapologetic about its essential grasping nature. And it was a view different than the one which had dominated the United Kingdom and to a degree the United States since the end of World War II.

At the core of Thatcherism was hostility to government meeting people's social needs—and scorn for the socialist elements that Britain had implemented in the postwar years. In her view, "I came to office with one deliberate intent: to change Britain from a dependent to a self-reliant society—from a give-it-to-me to a do-it-yourself nation. A get-up-and-go, instead of a sit-back-and-wait-for-it Britain."[30] Thatcher's simplistic tropes—which masked the true aim of her business-friendly political-economic doctrine—would soon be joined by those of Ronald Reagan. In Reagan's view, again employing dissembling sound bites, "Government is not the solution to our problem; government is the problem."[31] At the core of Thatcher's and Reagan's outlook was a philosophy that sought to end any significant role of government to meet social needs—from aiding affordable housing and providing healthcare to supporting the arts. And this was being done under the cover of promoting personal freedom and responsibility.

This political philosophy would come to be called neoliberalism, which David Harvey defines as "in the first instance a theory of political economic practices that proposes that human well-being can best be advanced by liberating individual entrepreneurial freedoms and skills within an institutional framework characterized by strong private property rights, free markets, and free trade. The role of the state is to create and preserve an institutional framework appropriate to such practices."[32] Put crassly, the government should support those who are in the business of expanding capital. For everyone else, if you don't have money, or the wherewithal to otherwise make do, you are on your own.

While neoliberalism was taking concrete political form in 1979, its roots lay in an anti-communist ideology developed at the end of World War II by the Austrian political philosopher Friedrich von Hayek and others in the Mont Pelerin Society (named after the

Swiss resort where they met). That group's statement of aims would become a manifesto of sorts, arguing that "the position of the individual and the voluntary group are progressively undermined by extensions of arbitrary power."[33] As such, it stood in opposition to the nominal socialism existing in countries grouped around the Soviet Union, as well as the semi-socialized elements in places such as the United Kingdom and France.

Hayek and his colleagues' ideas—incubated in the fever days of the Cold War—would find a more welcoming audience among the ruling elites as the final phase of that struggle got underway.

## Chrysler Gets a Reprieve

The tenets of neoliberalism were on sharp display when the country's tenth-largest corporation, Chrysler, faced the prospect of going out of business after recording losses of $1.1 billion.[34] The crisis sent the company, hat in hand, to the government for relief. The government obliged. The result was the 1979 Chrysler Loan Guarantee Act, which provided $1.5 billion in loans to the faltering company.[35] Despite the energy crisis, a recession, and proclamations of austerity by the Federal Reserve, the government, in the case of Chrysler, saw its role as a benefactor.

The popular conception of the Chrysler bailout is that it was the result of pressure from the United Auto Workers and the lobbying of representatives of local car dealerships, who pressured a recalcitrant Congress to step in and help. While there is some truth in this, there was another issue at play. More than any industry, auto was iconic of U.S. manufacturing predominance in the world. However, as the seventies progressed it was increasingly taking a hit from Japanese and German automakers, suggesting that dominance was coming to an end. To a degree then, this was about saving a symbolic U.S. industry as a way of reinforcing national prestige. However, the bailout was also a real-world application of neoliberalism. The government stepping in with a massive bailout for a corporation—such money could have easily been put toward creating jobs or social programs—was in keeping with the neoliberal view that the government was there not to help people struggling to survive but to be the eager assistant in all matters of "property rights, free markets, and free trade." Chrysler was emblematic of all that.

In October 1979, the economist Paul Volcker took over as head of the country's central bank, the U.S. Federal Reserve. On assuming the position, he initiated a policy to combat inflation, a program that meant higher interest rates. The effect, not unexpectedly, was to make a bad situation worse for most people in the country. In short order, the economy again went into a recession, one that would persist—with only brief interludes of growth—for several years.[36]

On the surface, the action of the Federal Reserve seemed a matter of short-term hard choices in order to get things back on track for the long haul. Looking deeper, however, it was indicative of the United States leaving for good the salad days of post–World War II affluence. Gone would be the time when a large share of the population—many with only a high school education—could enjoy a robust middle-class life. While this was not a falling off of a cliff, things had entered a downward—if elongated—spiral.[37] As *Washington Post* columnist Nancy Rosse wrote, "As the Sobering Seventies ended, the party was over for a generation, drunk on the almighty dollar and American invincibility. The Me Decade, still incredulous that the music had stopped, staggered into the chilling dawn of the Eighties."[38]

# 5

# China on the Capitalist Road

On the proposal of our great leader
Chairman Mao, the Political Bureau
unanimously agrees to dismiss
Deng Xiaoping from all posts both
inside and outside the Party while
allowing him to keep his Party
membership so as to see how he
will behave in the future.

—THE CENTRAL COMMITTEE OF THE
COMMUNIST PARTY OF CHINA,
April 1976

Deng Xiaoping entered the seventies as a political exile, kept from
the center of power since the fury days of the Cultural Revolution.
Deng's sin—such as things were in Maoist China—was to be too
closely aligned with a prime target of that event Liu Shaoqi, who

had been branded as "the biggest capitalist roader in the Party." In the mid-seventies, however, the twists and turns of the Cultural Revolution—which had upended nearly every aspect of Chinese society—were coming to an end. Mao would soon be dead and new leadership was consolidating itself. At the head of it was Deng Xiaoping.

## The Cultural Revolution and After

Between 1966 and 1976, the People's Republic of China was engaged in a rolling series of upheavals called the Great Proletarian Cultural Revolution (GPCR)—an undertaking whose proclaimed aims were to prevent the restoration of capitalism in that country. The initiative, which saw millions of young people denouncing once-venerated leaders, led to factionalism, violence, and near societal collapse. As Mao Zedong characterized things, "For several years there was chaos under heaven, fighting in various places throughout the nation, widespread civil war."[1]

Mao had set loose the turmoil in 1966, with his proclamation "It's right to rebel," a slogan aimed at dislodging entrenched conservative Party officials. Heading into the seventies, however, Mao was attempting to steer the country on a path of moderation, while retaining the relatively radical socialist character of the country. In doing this, he and those around him cautioned about the implications of failure: "Our country at present practices a commodity system, the wage system is unequal too, as in the eight-grade wage scale, and so forth. Under the dictatorship of the proletariat such things can only be restricted. Therefore, if people like Lin Piao come to power, it will be quite easy for them to rig up the capitalist system."[2] That explanation was popularized amid a criticism campaign that followed the death of Mao's chosen successor, Lin Biao. In 1971, Lin died in a plane crash, which according to the government was en route to the Soviet Union.

Lin's death had thrown everything about the GPCR into the air, and the left leadership in the Communist Party was trying mightily to cast his attempt to flee to the Soviet Union, China's chief adversary at the time, as emblematic of his embrace of "revisionism"—the disparaging label for counterrevolution. At the same time, achieving some measure of stability in running the country, involved bringing back some of the people who had previously been deposed. Among them was Deng, who came out of political exile in 1973. As things turned out, his re-emergence would be short lived.

In February 1976, in the wake of the death of Premier Zhou Enlai, Deng again became a target of political criticism. The precipitating incident occurred in early April, during Qingming, China's traditional day of mourning. On that occasion thousands came to Tiananmen Square to pay tribute to the dead premier, feeling his death had not been properly acknowledged. In China, such public displays were politically charged. As such, mourning Zhou was seen as a rebellion against the left-wing faction of Party leaders.

What followed was a confrontation, with mourners demanding to be heard and Party leadership insisting things end. Matters escalated. Amid criticisms by the far-left politburo members who would come to be called "the Gang of Four," an order was given to clear the square of memorials to Zhou. This in turn led to more aggressive protests, ending up in a riot. In its aftermath, Deng was accused of organizing the incident—now branded a counterrevolutionary action. With the backing of Mao, Deng was once again sent into the political wilderness.[3] That exile would be short, however. On September 9, 1976, just over five months after the Tiananmen incident, Mao died, paving the way for Deng's reinstatement.

Initially, Hua Guofeng, Mao's choice as successor, became the new head of the Chinese Communist Party. One of Hua's first acts as leader was to dispatch the far-left politburo members. To that end, he ordered the arrest of the Gang of Four—Jiang

Qing (Mao's wife), Zhang Chunqiao, Wang Hongwen, and Yao Wenyuan. They were then made the target of yet another national campaign. This time the focus was not on revisionism, but ultraleftism.

The purging of the Gang of Four was a highly consequential historic act. It was the first step in challenging the unquestioned authority of Mao Zedong—whose support for the Four had allowed them to wield influence. It also, relatedly, set China on a course toward a market economy, or what the Chinese would come to call "socialism with Chinese characteristics." As counterintuitive as this sounds, it was not as difficult as it might at first seem. As Maurice Meisner explains: "At the end of the Mao period, China contained elements of both socialism and capitalism—but without either being essentially socialist or capitalist. The hybrid character of the Mao regime reflected the contradiction between the bourgeois and socialist aspects of the Chinese revolution, a contradiction that Mao Zedong's successors would inherit."[4] Given that, and in line with their predilection for a robust economy over everything, the Communist Party leadership set a course toward developing the dynamic elements of capitalism. To that end, Hua and those grouped around him promoted what they called "the four modernizations"—a term that called for the rapid advancement of agriculture, industry, national defense, and science and technology. China was aiming to "be transformed into a powerful, modern socialist country by the end of the century."[5]

Once the new course was set, things rapidly shifted, including amid the political leadership. Deng, who had been restored to a powerful position, would soon replace Hua Guofeng.[6] The event that enshrined Deng as the pre-eminent leader, was the 3rd Plenary of the Party's 11th Central Committee, which met in December 1978.[7] That plenary issued a communique that laid out the priorities for the country and the Party: "Carrying out the four modernizations requires great growth in the productive forces, which in turn requires a diverse change in those aspects of the relations of production and the superstructure not in harmony with the growth of the productive forces, and requires changes in all methods of management, actions, and thinking which stand in the way of such growth."[8] Setting aside the socialist jargon, this was a call to accelerate production and economic growth. As such, enshrining the four modernizations into the Party's political line signaled a rapid shift toward production, over everything else.

The plenary came on the heels of the previous two years' shifting of priorities away from a popular socialism toward a more capitalist sensibility. A sense of this comes through in articles that appeared in the weekly *Peking Review*. For example, one piece was rhetorically titled "Can an Enterprise Be Run without Rules and Regulations?" In the piece's view, Lin Biao and the Gang of Four wrongly considered rules and regulations as implements for "controlling, curbing and suppressing the working class." Quoting Zhou Enlai, the piece asserted that while such measures were very much in need, "rational rules and regulations must be improved." Another article was entitled "Observe Economic Laws: Speed Up the Four Modernizations." This was a none-too-veiled argument against the Maoist concept of putting radical socialist politics in command as a way of advancing economically—and in everything else.[9] Also during this time, Hua Guofeng gave a much publicized speech at the National Finance and Trade Conference on Learning from Taching and Tachai (two models of development in China's agriculture), where he proclaimed the need to "catch up with and surpass the economic and technical levels of the most advanced capitalist countries."[10]

While it can be argued that the Maoist principles being countered were fraught in many ways, driven by no small amount of voluntarism—what was being undertaken was an all-out negation of what had been in place during Mao's rule, not a simple course correction. China was hurtling toward a production model based on accelerated and efficient production and constant growth—the sine qua non of a capitalist economy.

## Democracy Wall

A key problem for Deng and the other Chinese leaders as they embarked on this path was how to undo Mao's legacy—which argued for development aimed at curtailing rather than exacerbating capitalist dynamics—in a situation in which most living Chinese had been told relentlessly over the previous decade that Mao's thinking was sacrosanct. Speaking with the Italian journalist Oriana Fallaci, Deng Xiaoping laid out his approach on how to see Mao:

> We shall certainly evaluate Chairman Mao's merits and mistakes which characterized his life. We shall certainly affirm his merits and say that they are of primary importance, acknowledge his errors and assess that they are secondary, and while making them public we will adopt a realistic attitude. But, also, we shall certainly continue to uphold Mao Tse-tung Thought, which was the correct part of his life. No, it isn't only his portrait which remains in Tiananmen Square: It is the memory of a man who guided us to victory and built a country. Which is far from being little. And for this, the Chinese Communist Party and the Chinese people will always cherish him as a very valuable treasure. Do write this: We shall not do to Mao Tse-tung what Khrushchev did to Stalin at the 20th Soviet Communist Party Congress.[11]

Put another way, they would not undertake a scorched earth policy on Mao and thoroughly discredit him—though they would reject the greater part of Mao's conception of what a socialist society ought to be. To that end, while they would allow some criticism of him, they would hang greater weight of enmity on his radical supporters.[12]

With regard to the latter, the view was to take no prisoners. In the national campaign to vilify the Gang of Four, there was a special venom reserved for Mao's wife, Jiang Qing—someone whom

Deng had a personal hatred of. Here is how he contrasts Mao with Jiang Qing, "Listen, when I say that Chairman Mao made, mistakes, I also think of the mistake named Jiang Qing. She is a very, very evil woman. She is so evil that any evil thing you say about her isn't evil enough, and if you ask me to judge her with the grades as we do in China, I answer that this is impossible, there are no grades for Jiang Qing, that Jiang Qing is a thousand times a thousand below zero." Free of all previous constraints, Deng was, as they say, letting it all hang out.

The problem, however, was that it was Mao who was ultimately responsible for Deng and the other leaders' rise and fall. He was the only one in the most tumultuous years of the Cultural Revolution who had unquestioned power—knocking him down would be perilous. To Deng's point about Khrushchev denouncing Stalin, Maurice Meisner notes, "To simply denounce Mao as a tyrant and enumerate his tyrannies to explain the evils of the past as Nikita Khrushchev had denounced Stalin . . . would have risked calling into question not only the political legitimacy of the Chinese Communist State but the moral validity of the revolution that produced it."[13] In approaching the matter of criticizing Mao, the fundamental legitimacy of Chinese society and government was at stake.

To address this, one mechanism the leadership settled on was to allow a period of openness, where Mao could be challenged in a way that did not appear to come from the government. This happened by way of the Party's tacit support of displaying big-character posters—a form dating to the early days of the Cultural Revolution—which allowed controversial opinions to be made public.

As a result, in November 1978, posters started appearing on a wall near Beijing's Tiananmen Square. The topics ranged widely from personal grievances to mistreatment by government authorities. There was even a poster challenging the dominant policy of delayed marriage and delayed love: "It's a cruel crime that destroys young hearts and bodies."[14] Amid these were posters that were more consequential.

Controversially, and going to the core reason the displays were tolerated, were missives that challenged Mao's assessment of the Cultural Revolution. One posting extolled Deng's benefactor, Liu Shaoqi, with a foot-tall headline proclaiming "Liu Shaoqi is eternal." Another posting audaciously criticized Mao directly: "Mao did not create New China, it was the revolution that created Mao."[15] A few years earlier such declarations would be taken as apostasy, but they now were openly allowed.

Those elements were more or less welcomed by the authorities, given the need to move the Chinese public away from its near-religious fealty to Mao's outlook. However, the limits of the liberalization were clear, as can be seen in the response to a poster signed by an entity called "The Human Rights Group," which implored Jimmy Carter to extend his human rights campaign to China. Not only was the entry met with comments calling it "shameful" and "dirty," it contrasted the United States to China, asking if the group wanted "the sort of democracy that led to last month's mass suicide-murder by members of the California-based Peoples Temple in Guyana."[16] The posting was also criticized directly by Deng: "The so-called China Human Rights Organization has even tacked up big character posters requesting the American president 'to show solicitude' toward human rights in China. Can we permit these kinds of public demands for foreigners to interfere in China's domestic affairs? A so-called Thaw Society issued a proclamation openly opposing the dictatorship of the proletariat, saying that it divided people. Can we permit this kind of 'freedom of speech,' which openly opposes constitutional principles?"[17] The rulers of China were not going to allow the authority of the Party to be challenged, let alone have the United States meddling in their affairs.

Not surprisingly, the opening was short lived. In December 1979, authorities banned posters from the Xidan Wall, a side street of Tiananmen Square in the center of Beijing. They redirected any postings to Uetan Park, in a residential neighborhood three miles from the Xidan site. Along with the geographical marginalization, the government stipulated that any postings on the site would

Deng Xiaoping in Houston. Photo: NASA (U.S. Government).

require people to register their names, pseudonyms, addresses, and workplaces.[18] Anonymity was not going to be allowed. The days of openness were at an end.

Regardless, this was part of softening up China's population for a dramatic shift toward the feverous pursuit of growth.[19] An article in *Peking Review* pointedly underscored the new priorities. Prominently featured on the cover of an August 1978 issue was an article titled "Implementing the Socialist Principle 'To Each according to His Work.'" Ostensibly expounding on Marx's definition of socialism, the piece omitted Marx's larger point that under socialism there was inequality, and it was only a stepping-stone to a communist society where the principle was to be "from each according to his ability, to each according to his need."[20] China was in a hurry to exalt the first and in no hurry to talk about the second. As one press account presciently noted, "[Mao's] successors have set as their goal nothing less than the economic and physical transformation of the Chinese mainland. If they have their way, China will catch up with the industrialized world by the year 2000 and take its place among the world's great powers."[21] As things developed, this assessment was shown to be not only an accurate account of that country's aims but a historically accurate prediction.

These transformations were received in the United States with something akin to jubilation. In January 1979, Deng was anointed "Man of the Year" by the historically anti-communist *Time* magazine. When he visited the country that same month he was greeted as royalty. He was feted by Jimmy Carter at the White House, toured the headquarters of Coca-Cola in Atlanta, was photographed playfully wearing a cowboy hat in Texas, and visited a Boeing assembly plant in Washington state. The red carpet had been rolled out. This was in stark contrast to the relationship the United States had had with China since 1949 when the former engaged the latter in a shooting war in Korea, threatened it with nuclear weapons in the mid-1950s, and denounced it as a pariah state beyond the pale in the 1960s.[22] All of that was in the past. A new, capitalist-friendly China was emerging on the world stage.

# 6

# Up against
# the Wall

It's gonna be a battle, it's gonna be
a struggle, it's gonna be a leap, and
we can, we must, and we will make
it. Because you see, the times are
sharpening up.

—**BOB AVAKIAN**, chairman of the
Revolutionary Communist Party,
USA, 1979

A staple of media fare as the fervor of the sixties was replaced by the
relative calm of the seventies were tales of former radicals surfacing
and surrendering. The examples were pointed, if selective, but the
message was clear: the days of insurrectionary dreams were over.
There was, for example, Eldridge Cleaver, the fiery leader of the
Black Panther Party. Cleaver had once challenged Ronald Reagan
to a duel, saying, "I will beat him to death with a marshmallow,

cause he's a punk." Cleaver had fled the country in 1969 after a shootout with Oakland police and returned to the United States after seven years in exile in Algeria. He was, it turned out, ready to leave any trace of radicalism behind.[1] He made news in 1975 pitching a line of men's pants with a codpiece, his aim being to market a product counter to unisex or "sissy-pants."[2]

In a similar vein, there was Yippie Jerry Rubin, an uber-radical whose 1970 book *Do It!: Scenarios of the Revolution* contained a two-page graphic with letters blaring "Fuck Amerika." In it, he wrote, "The money-economy is immoral, based totally on power and manipulation, offending the natural exchange between human beings." As the seventies ended, Rubin found work at the Wall Street firm of John Muir & Co.—a position he assumed amid a boisterous PR campaign promoting his shift from radical to entrepreneur.[3]

Then there was LSD guru Timothy Leary. It was Leary who popularized the maxim "turn on, tune in, drop out." By 1970, he found himself in San Luis Obispo prison in California on a drug conviction. A year later the radical Weathermen—keen to bolster their counterculture bona fides—broke him out of prison, secreting him to Algeria by way of Cuba to join members of the Black Panther Party who were in exile there. Unfortunately, Leary and his Panther hosts did not get along. By 1972 he was living in Afghanistan when he was seized by authorities. On his return to the United States, he agreed to inform on those who helped him escape. Despite such cooperation, he soon found himself interred in the less escapable Folsom Prison.[4]

There was also Black Panther leader Huey Newton, whom the left had fought so mightily to free. In 1974, he was accused of pistol-whipping his tailor and of killing a seventeen-year-old prostitute in a separate incident. As a result, he fled to Cuba, returning to the United States in 1977 to face the charges. While the 1978 assault and 1979 murder trials resulted in hung juries, he was convicted of a weapons possession charge in the tailor case, a violation of his parole. He would return to prison in 1981.[5]

And there was Rennie Davis, an anti-war leader who became famous as a defendant in the Chicago 7 conspiracy trial, who turned to the worship of a fifteen-year-old guru.[6] There were others, duly publicized, with the message hammered home that the sixties are done, your icons have crumbled—it's over.

Complicating that storyline was the fact that the majority of those radicalized in the preceding decade had not undertaken such discordant transformations. Most, in fact, had attempted to retain some measure of social justice integrity—if on their own unique terms—people such as Tom Hayden, Abbie Hoffman, Daniel Ellsberg, Joan Baez, Jane Fonda, David Dillinger, and millions of lesser-known others. Beyond such people, however, were a small but not insignificant number who held tight to their radicalism. And it was these forces, amid profound changes in the United States and globally, who found themselves struggling to find their way in a far different world than the one that had birthed them.

## The Challenge for U.S. Maoists

While Deng Xiaoping's tour of the United States was for him, a triumph, for Maoists in the United States it was an affront. The Revolutionary Communist Party, USA (RCP) had entered the seventies—then called the Revolutionary Union—as the most coherent radical communist organization to traverse the rocks and sinkholes of the sixties. Unlike organizations such as the Yippies, Black Panthers, and Weathermen, who were in various states of decline in the early 1970s, the RCP had come through intact and organizationally cohesive.

Things were such that in September 1976 the FBI cast the group in ominous terms, proclaiming in a report that "the RCP, RSB [Revolutionary Student Brigade], and its front groups, identified as the VVAW [Vietnam Veterans Against the War], UWOC [Unemployed Workers Organizing Committee], and USCPFA [U.S. China People's Friendship Association], represent a threat to the internal security of the United States of the first magnitude."[7] That assessment came soon before the FBI was forced to scale back its domestic security operations to conform to the U.S. attorney general's new, more restrictive guidelines. When the 1976 report on the RCP was written, however, it reflected a real concern on the part of the FBI about a disciplined and sophisticated pro-Maoist group operating within the United States.

By the decade's end, however, the group was in crisis. At the end of 1977, they had undergone a major split, with those leaving supporting China's new leaders and those remaining opposing them. As a result, the RCP's numbers—a small but committed cadre of around a thousand—had been reduced by a third.

With Maoism itself under attack in China, the RCP was struggling to get its bearings. Rather than taking a more sober stock of the situation, they quickly consolidated around the slogan "Mao Zedong Did Not Fail, Revolution Will Prevail." In this way, they were able to step over large parts of the complicated situation in China—one made fraught in no small way by measures undertaken under Mao's leadership. What they arrived at instead was that Mao and the four politburo members, including Mao's widow Jiang Qing, were the real revolutionaries—and the current leaders of China were revisionist counterrevolutionaries. The immediate task then was to make this known around the world. The hope was, to the degree this was a worked-out strategy, that this would contribute to the ability of Chinese revolutionaries to reassert power somewhere down the road.

As such, when Deng visited Washington the group organized an ad hoc committee consisting of RCP cadres and close supporters called the Committee for a Fitting Welcome for Deng Xiaoping. Their first act was a symbolic assault on the Chinese chancery, soon to become the Chinese embassy. There, five men threw lead fishing weights at the windows and left an effigy of Deng on the steps of the building. Around the effigy's neck was a sign reading "Deng Xiaoping—Traitor Beware."[8]

Following the embassy action was a march of a few hundred to the White House where Jimmy Carter was feting Deng. The plan appears to have been to launch an array of objects in the direction of the White House, thus disrupting the official proceedings. However, that was pre-empted when a sizable mobilization of police blocked any effort by the group to get close enough to the presidential mansion. Frustrated, the group proceeded to hurl various objects at the police. The police in turn responded, with disproportionate brutality. As the *Washington Post* described the incident: "[RCP demonstrators] broke into a run, shouting 'Death, Death to Teng Hsiaoping' and began hurtling bottles, poles, lighted flares, and hundreds of nails, heavy washers, and fishing sinkers at both D.C. and U.S. Park police.... Police, apparently caught off guard quickly recovered and with reinforcements charged into the crowd, swinging their clubs wildly."[9] The result was a brief, if bloody, melee. In all, seventy-eight demonstrators were arrested. Initially, they were held on misdemeanor riot charges—the tenor by authorities being to dispense with this without making it a major case. However, within a couple of days, the government's view shifted with the appearance in court of Earl Silbert, a former Watergate prosecutor. Silbert escalated charges up to felony assault on a police officer on all those arrested. The arrestees now faced a possible five-year prison sentence and were held on $10,000 bail.[10]

As the government further reviewed their evidence, they winnowed the case down to seventeen defendants, including the group's leader, Bob Avakian, who was charged with multiple felonies. As a result, the RCP, which had traversed the period of the late sixties into the seventies staying inside legal lines, now found themselves confronting serious judicial peril. That danger included charges against their leader, who in a worst-case scenario faced decades in prison. This would condition the group's behavior going forward, including Avakian leaving the country and residing overseas for decades.

## The Communist Workers Party

The RCP was not alone in its conviction that the situation in the United States was on the cusp of radical, even revolutionary, tumult. While the RCP's size and influence were at best modest, the Workers Viewpoint Organization (WVO), another Maoist entity, was several steps below that.[11]

The WVO had evolved out of something called the Asian Study Group in New York City, founded in 1971 by a former State University of New York Stony Brook student and member of the Maoist Progressive Labor Party, Jerry Tung. The group drew its membership mainly from New York's City College and the city's Chinatown neighborhood. As their name implies, their work revolved largely around study, particularly the works of Marx, Lenin, and Mao. That dogmatic disposition never fully disappeared. They did, however, attempt to expand beyond a study circle into organizing among the "proletariat." As such, in 1974 they renamed themselves the Workers Viewpoint Organization. Three years later, like several other small groups aiming to consolidate forces and establish themselves as a "new communist party," they renamed themselves again: this time to the Communist Workers Party (CWP).[12]

While their size and influence were small, by the late seventies the CWP became notable in certain circles for its outsize bravado and penchant for confrontation. This was on sharp display in North Carolina, where they were focusing their work in the textile industry—particularly in the Cone Mill plant in Greensboro.

## Sectarian Targets

The story of the CWP's defining crisis is bound up with the state of the new communist left in 1979. These forces confronted a situation in which their revolutionary aspirations butted up against the fact that their model, Maoist China, was slowly but surely turning to dust. Some took this as a cue to direct their work in more restrained directions. But like the RCP, the CWP redoubled their efforts toward a more imminent communist revolution, lashing out against real and perceived enemies of that project. This included not only factory owners, white supremacists, and government authorities, but their competitors in the ultra-left, including the RCP.

In the wake of the anti-Deng demonstration, the RCP organized a national speaking tour for Bob Avakian, this to up his profile and build support for his legal case. One of the stops on the tour, in October 1979, was Greensboro. The CWP responded to this as an invasion of their turf. As such, they confronted RCP partisans leafleting at the North Carolina Agricultural and Technical University homecoming parade. A scuffle ensued. According to the RCP's press, "These WVO goons slashed at them with razor blades, maced them, and grunted, 'You better get out of town and stay out.'"[13] After Avakian's speech, another group of RCP leafleteers, this time at the White Oak textile factory, were again confronted by CWP cadres and supporters. According to the RCP's sensational account, "These reactionaries came out of the plant armed with bricks and outnumbered the leafleteers 2 to 1. One leafleteer was put in the hospital as a result of this pig attack." For their part, CWP offered their own breathless account, accusing "twelve RCP 'cowards, armed with spiked clubs' of attacking two White Oak workers."[14]

Such confrontations, as serious as they were, were not the only preoccupations of the CWP in this period. They also set their sights on a far more lethal adversary—organized white supremacists.

## Confrontation and Confusion in China Grove

In the summer of 1979, the CWP learned of a showing of the racist film *Birth of a Nation* (1915) scheduled in the town of China Grove, a small village sixty miles to the east of Greensboro. To challenge what they saw as a racist provocation, they sent a squad of people to disrupt the showing. While their action was boisterous, it was not especially violent, though in the course of their disruption they ripped down a Confederate flag. The confrontation ended when police convinced the Klansmen present to retreat into the building where the film showing would take place. While that action ended without any injuries, it set in motion things far more tragic.

Notably, events in China Grove, among other things, appear to have caused confusion for the white supremacists who had been targeted. This is clear from the National Socialist Party of America (NSPA)'s newsletter of August 1979. The cover, which shows armed white supremacists in China Grove, reads: "On July 8th, members of the NSPA Forsyth County Unit assisted the Federated Knights of the Ku Klux Klan at a showing of the 1915 film, 'Birth of a Nation' in China Grove, N.C. The meeting was attacked by about 60 members of the Revolutionary Communist Party, but the reds were repulsed by NSPA Stormtroopers and Klan Security Guards."[15] The most notable thing here—putting aside their confusing the CWP for the RCP—is that the white supremacists saw fit to record the incident in their press and spin a narrative favorable to them, suggesting they were particularly stung by the incident.

## Bluster and Tragedy in Greensboro

At the end of October 1979, the WVO transformed into the CWP. At its founding conference, the group's leader Jerry Tung spoke of the imminence of revolution, proclaiming "This is the beginning of our countdown."[16] One of the group's first acts as the CWP would be a demonstration on November 3, in a march and rally calling for "Death to the Klan."

The rhetoric in advance of the demonstration was incendiary. In the lead-up, to the march, CWP member Paul Bermanzohn released a statement directed at the white supremacists. In part, it read: "They [the Klan] must be physically beaten back, eradicated, exterminated, wiped off the face of the earth. We invite you and your two-bit punks to come and face the wrath of the people."[17] The white supremacists accepted the challenge.

On the Saturday of the march, Klansmen and Nazis traveled in a nine-car caravan to the demonstration site. On arrival one of the Klansmen is reported to have said, "You wanted the Klan, here we are!" When some among the demonstrators began to beat on their cars with the thick sticks that held their placards, things escalated. The white supremacists, who had brought a small arsenal with them, opened fire on the demonstrators. A few of the protestors had brought weapons and attempted to defend themselves, but they were wildly outgunned.[18] Compounding and effectively facilitating the violence was the absence of the Greensboro police, who did not arrive on the scene until after the carnage.

When the shooting stopped at least ten people were wounded and four of the demonstrators, Caesar Cauce, Sandra Smith, Will Sampson, and Jim Waller, lay dead. Michael Nathan, who was critically wounded—would die two days later. It was a horrible, one-sided slaughter, one in which the police, by their absence, objectively aided the white supremacists.

In the wake of the killings, the CWP, justifiably outraged, urged people from around the country to come to the funeral. However, the call, in hyperbolic language and unsubstantiated conspiracy theorizing, was limiting: "With living standards worsening and confidence in the government shattering, the American people are waking up. The U.S. bourgeoisie is using selective repression against the mounting resistance of the working class. The murder of these comrades by agents of the government is an attack on all working and oppressed people in this country. Panicking, the bourgeoisie struck out—but they've unleashed a movement more militant, more determined, and more massive than they ever dreamed."[19] Given such questionable analysis, and the modest support CWP had, it is not surprising the turnout for the march was small. Authorities, expecting a large crowd, had mobilized a force of close to a thousand state troopers, National Guard members, and local police. However, at most five hundred people took part—with police and media outnumbering them. It was a showing hardly commensurate with the magnitude of the crime.[20] Compounding this, news of the killings was almost immediately overshadowed by events in Iran, where students seized the U.S. embassy in Tehran the day after the killings.

## Confrontation in Powelton Village

The group MOVE was not a radical organization in a conventional leftist sense. Begun in Philadelphia in the early seventies, it was a communal, multiracial, back-to-nature, anti-establishment entity. It was the latter aspect, which included a lifestyle that eschewed conventional norms and readily involved confrontations and obscenity-laden harangues—this in the starkly polarized black-white city of Philadelphia—that vaulted them into the headlines and made them a focus of governmental and police attention. A sense of this comes through in the fact that after appearing on the scene only around 1974, by 1978 the tiny group was reported to have been involved in up to 250 trials for various run-ins and confrontations with authorities.[21]

In the spring and summer of 1978, matters came to a head. In March of that year, city officials, led by the hardline and notoriously brutal former police chief Mayor Frank Rizzo, laid siege to the group's home in the Powelton Village neighborhood near the University of Pennsylvania—one of the few integrated neighborhoods in the city. At issue, according to the city, was the unsanitary conditions, which neighbors had complained about. In response to the complaints, the group first refused a proper inspection and then declined to leave after ostensibly negotiating their departure to a farm in Virginia.[22]

The standoff remained unresolved until August 8, when at 5:30 A.M. the city unleashed an offensive on the group's home. They began by systematically towing all the parked vehicles in the proximity of the house. Then, at 6:04 A.M., they blasted orders via bullhorn to those inside to vacate. Ten minutes later, a bulldozer driven by a riot-helmeted policeman knocked down a wooden barricade built by MOVE to protect the front of the house, taking a part of the porch with it. A few minutes later a construction cherry picker was used as a battering ram to punch out the boarded-up windows and knock holes in the building. Then police began pumping thousands of gallons of water into the house through high-pressure hoses.

The siege, nonetheless, continued for a couple of hours, with the group refusing to exit. Then the police, claiming someone inside had fired shots at them, opened fire. When the shooting stopped one of their officers was dead—police claiming it was the result of MOVE. MOVE, however, would say the death was the result of the police's own firing. Regardless, the fusillade of bullets brought matters to an end.

While the matter of who shot the officer—James Ramp— remained disputed, one thing was not. In images caught by the media, MOVE member Delbert Africa, emerging from the building with his hands raised in surrender, was knocked to the ground, viciously kicked, and slammed with a riot helmet by three police officers on the scene.[23]

The city's final action, now that the MOVE members and their children were in custody, was to remove any vestiges of the group's presence in the neighborhood. A crane, which residents had thought was part of a construction project at nearby Drexel University, quickly moved into position, along with bulldozers, and proceeded to raze the residence to the ground, leaving only a vacant lot.[24] The action, as one lawyer pointed out, constituted "obliterating evidence."[25] City officials, were more intent on delivering a message than preserving a crime scene.

Compounding this, in December 1979 nine MOVE members were put on trial, accused of the murder of Officer Ramp. Opting for trial in front of a judge, rather than a jury, the confrontations continued, this time via disruptions by the MOVE defendants in the courtroom. The judge threatened to gag them and later to clear them from the court. All nine would be convicted the following year and given jail terms ranging from thirty to a hundred years.[26]

While all these groups had their particularities and the outcomes of their crises were in no way equal, they did share a certain view that a critical moment was at hand—one that demanded no compromise. While the authorities responded with brutal and disproportionate power—or in the case of the Nazis and the Klan, murder—one cannot escape the fact that such millenarian views served those who held them poorly. That all of this was getting expressed in the final year of the decade was, in hindsight, hardly a surprise. Big changes were coming that would radically reorient nearly everything, though not in the way such forces hoped.[27]

# 7

# The Use of
# Terrorism

Because hard-core terrorists are
relatively isolated, they can be dealt
with primarily as a police problem.

—**WILLIAM B. QUANDT**, the Brookings
Institution, 1985

While the political radicals of the RCP and CWP straddled the
line of legality in 1979—and as a result were met with escalating
repression—forces who had adopted political violence as their rai-
son d'être were presented with an even harsher situation. The period
saw them confront a far less animated political terrain than the one
from which they had emerged. As such, they saw shrinking numbers and a dwindling base of support. Despite this, they retained a
small hard core. Unfortunately, their efforts—meant to inspire and
motivate the masses to "bring down Babylon"—only worked to
drive them further into the underground where they had taken

refuge. This in turn further constrained their ability to act in any politically meaningful way. It also, if unintentionally, contributed to the government's ability to sharpen and develop new repressive instruments as a by-product of their pursuit of them.

## The Weather Underground

As the sixties tumult was moving to a conclusion, small elements of the Black Panther Party (BPP), Students for a Democratic Society (SDS), and others among the hyper-radically inclined embarked on a road of political violence under the banner of urban guerilla warfare. The Weather Underground (WU) emerged from a split in SDS, the largest radical student organization of the sixties. The Weathermen were always a small entity, but they garnered outsize coverage in the media—which saw them as emblematic, and cautionary, of the larger radicalism. As such, they constituted a presence beyond their numbers and actual impact.

What is telling in this respect is that the action for which the group is most famous was not one that targeted the government but rather an accident that killed three of their own members. In March 1970, a team of Weatherpeople staying in a family member's Greenwich Village townhouse were constructing a bomb. The aim was to plant it at a noncommissioned officers' dance at Fort Dix, New Jersey. Fortunately for the personnel at Fort Dix, but tragically for the radicals, the bomb under construction exploded, killing Ted Gold, Diana Oughton, and Terry Robins. Another two members, Kathy Boudin and Cathy Wilkerson survived, running from the burning building to safety. These two were then able to continue their underground work.[1]

The second most famous action by the group was the planting of an explosive inside the restroom on the Senate side of the U.S. Capitol in March 1971. The explosion caused $300,000 in property damage but resulted in no human injuries. The bombing was carried out as a countermeasure to the Nixon administration's incursion into Laos. However, not only did it do nothing to stop the Laos incursion, the action also set the FBI loose against members of the Youth International Party, who had no part in the bombing and who were at that moment organizing for what would be the massive May 1971 demonstrations in Washington, DC.[2] As such, it could be argued that they created as much trouble for themselves—and the larger movement—as they did for their stated adversaries in the U.S. power structure.

Regardless, and in spite of their small size and influence, the WU were portrayed as a significant force on the American landscape. And while the media and certain politicians played up the threat posed by the group, the FBI—whose interests necessitated a more realistic assessment—had a different view internally: "Our investigation of the revolutionary Weathermen group centers on approximately 200 people throughout the country. Included in that number are the 26 Weathermen fugitives. Also included is a group of about 40 individuals, all non-fugitives, whose whereabouts are unknown and who are believed active in the Weather Underground." The report referred to them as "a small group . . . probably loosely coordinated," while concluding that they would "continue sporadic acts of extreme violence."[3]

That report was written in 1972. As the decade advanced, those small numbers became even smaller, with people leaving the movement and the underground behind. Among them was Mark Rudd, who had been a key figure in the Columbia University strike of 1968. In 1977, he turned himself in to face misdemeanor charges stemming from the group's 1969 "Days of Rage" demonstration in Chicago.[4] That demonstration, which took place while the group was still operating above ground, had as its slogan "Bring the War Home." The subsequent action saw a couple hundred demonstrators smash car and store windows and battle police in Chicago's Loop.[5] The demonstration's most lasting effect—aside from the outstanding warrants for those arrested who failed to appear in court—was to serve as a composite example for the dominant power structure of the futility of reckless radicalism.

Rudd's surfacing came at a time when the group had both an underground component and an above-ground support apparatus. In 1974, they published a manifesto titled *Prairie Fire: The Politics of Revolutionary Anti-Imperialism.* The publication was bylined by the most well-known Weatherpeople: Bill Ayers, Bernardine Dohrn, and Jeff Jones, along with Celia Sojourn—an apparent nom de guerre. While the document ran to more than 150 pages, covering issues from women's liberation to the Black freedom movement, what was perhaps most revealing about it was the statement of aims that unintentionally revealed the group's isolation: "Our intention is to disrupt the empire . . . to incapacitate it, to put pressure on the cracks, to make it hard to carry out its bloody functioning against the people of the world, to join the world struggle, to attack from the inside. Our intention is to encourage the people . . . to provoke leaps in confidence and consciousness, to stir the imagination, to popularize power, to agitate, to organize, to join in every way possible the people's day-to-day struggles."[6] It was a shopping list of objectives without much substance. As for joining "the people's day-to-day struggles," this was more fanciful than real. An organization of a few score "guerrillas," whose priority of necessity was evading arrest, could hardly be expected to exert much influence in above-ground politics.

That conflict lay at the base of an internal struggle. One section of the group wanted to surface to do more conventional organizing, while another wanted to continue with its previous model. The result led to a schism, with the expulsion of the former leadership— then based in New York—of Bill Ayers, Bernardine Dohrn, and Jeff Jones. In their place, Clayton Van Lydegraf, a sixty-two-year-old Communist Party veteran took charge. Notably, Van Lydegraf had grudgingly taken part in the escape of Timothy Leary. His tenure as leader of the WU, however, would not be long.

In 1977, Van Lydegraf, Judith Siff Bissell, Leslie Ann Mullin, Thomas M. Justeen, and Marc C. Perry were arrested in connection to a plot alleged to take place in Houston, Texas. The FBI claimed they were planning an elaborate campaign of terrorism, including targeting Judge Floyd Dotson, who presided over the trial of American Indian Movement activist Richard Skyhorse, and an effort against the anti-busing group "Bus Stop." However, rather than a dramatic trial, the government had to settle for a plea deal that saw all the defendants garner relatively modest three-year prison terms.

At his sentencing in 1979, Van Lydegraf denounced his jailing as politically motivated: "I have now been in jail for 1½ years with no trial, essentially for dangerous thoughts and political associations." While that may have been the case, and the FBI did put a lot of time and resources into tracking him down, his calling out the system went largely unnoticed. The fever days of the sixties had long since passed, and the judge in sentencing Van Lydegraf was withering: "It is a tragedy that five effective, intelligent persons should be involved . . . in such a waste of time which they could have devoted to some higher purpose."[7]

Those arrests effectively ended the Prairie Fire Organizing Committee, whose organization and leadership had concentrated on the West Coast. However, in New York, elements of the former WU would carry on as the May 19th Communist Organization—sans Dohrn, Ayers, and Jones, who would later surface apart from that group.[8] For the remaining hard core, however, the days of political violence-based activism were numbered.

## The Black Liberation Army

The WU was an organization comprised mainly of former white student radicals. By contrast, the Black Liberation Army (BLA) emerged from elements of the fraying BPP and the radical Black nationalist organization, Republic of New Afrika (RNA).[9]

The BPP, in particular, was always a complex phenomenon, a mix of radical politics, Black nationalism, and street organization.[10] Rather than a coherent national organization—which is how it is generally portrayed—it was more akin to a loose network of groupings in various cities, each with their own dynamics. This was on pronounced display in their New York chapter.

In the sixties and early seventies, the New York BPP had been singled out for harsh repression by the New York Police Department (NYPD), whose intelligence division (then known as the Bureau of Special Services and Investigations or BOSSI) had key informants within the group. In one of the most famous trials of the early seventies, twenty-one members of the New York chapter were accused of an elaborate plot to bomb department stores and police stations, and to murder police. The government's case, which revolved around NYPD undercover informants Gene Roberts and Ralph White, was by most measures a farce. It took a jury less than a day to acquit all the defendants—this in a trial that had lasted eight months.

Among the defendants in the case, however, was a cohort who would later align with or support political violence—this was in opposition to the reformism advocated by the BPP in Oakland after Huey P. Newton's release from prison in 1970. The cohort included Dhoruba al-Mujahid bin Wahad (formerly Richard Moore) and Michael Tabor, who had jumped bail and fled to Algeria to join Eldridge Cleaver rather than attend their trial. Bin Wahad would return to the United States—Tabor would remain out of the country—but was arrested in 1971 for a robbery. He was then charged and convicted, on specious evidence, of the murder of a police officer.[11] Also among the twenty-one were Kuwasi Balagoon (Donald Weems) and Sundiata Acoli (Clark Edward Squire) both of whom would figure into actions associated with the BLA.[12] Not included among the Panther 21, but a key figure in the New York chapter, was Assata Shakur (Joanne Chesimard). It was she whom authorities would claim headed the BLA.

The Panther 21 trial was fading into history in May 1973 when Assata Shakur, Sundiata Acoli, and Zayd Malik Shakur (James F. Coston, former information minister for Eldridge Cleaver) were stopped on the New Jersey Turnpike by state police. What ensued was a firefight in which Trooper Werner Foerster was shot and killed. His partner, James Harper, was also shot but survived. Also killed in the gun battle was Zayd Malik Shakur. Assata Shakur, shot in both arms and her shoulder, was taken into custody. Sundiata Acoli, who was able to flee the scene, was caught the next day.[13]

The incident on the New Jersey Turnpike would lay the basis for one of the most successful actions the BLA would claim credit for.

## Prison Break in Clinton

While Assata Shakur survived the New Jersey Turnpike shooting, she would be convicted for the killing of Werner Foerster—though her actual role remains in question. Regardless, in 1979 she was serving a life sentence in New Jersey's Clinton Correctional Facility. It was a sentence the BLA cut short when they broke her out of prison.

The escape was carried out with the aid of three men identified as members of the BLA along with a white supporter—said to be part of the WU. The men, using false identities, came to the prison ostensibly as visitors. Clinton, the only women's prison in New Jersey, had no walls or fencing around its perimeter, making it a far more accessible target than a conventional maximum security facility. The armed men—no one had searched them—entered the shuttle to take them to the prison and took two guards hostage, enabling them to free Shakur. They then fled by way of two awaiting cars.

From there what followed was a mix of hiding out and going into exile. Shakur first hid out in Pittsburgh until August 1980. She then traveled to the Bahamas. From there she made her way to Cuba, where she remained.[14]

At a later trial of Marilyn Buck—the white woman accused of helping to organize the prison break—a government witness, Tyron Rison, was asked why the group undertook the action. His response

Assata Shakur/Joanne Chesimard, 1977. Source: FBI (U.S. Government).

was telling. "We felt that just robbing Brink's trucks or guards or banks wasn't totally what we were about. It was time to do something that was totally political."[15] While Rison, a cooperating witness, is hardly the group's authoritative source, his statement is nonetheless revealing. With a shrinking base of support commensurate with the ebb in the turmoil of earlier years, these would-be revolutionaries were forced to rely on illegal acts—they called them "expropriations"—to survive. In other words, by the end of the seventies, the line between guerilla operations and outright criminality had faded to gray. More pointedly, it foretold that a certain kind of radicalism was at an end. Faded or not, it left a legacy—if an unintended one.

## From Internal Security to Terrorism

While these urban guerillas were carrying out their strategies, the authorities seized on the opportunity to sharpen their repressive instruments. While pursuing radical organizations operating within the law presented limitations on what could openly be brought to bear against them, that was not the case regarding those who had broken U.S. laws. Those actions allowed law enforcement to use every tool in their considerable arsenal.

By the end of the seventies, the FBI and NYPD were evolving a new mechanism for pursuing forces deemed terrorists—groups such as the BLA, WU, May 19th Communist Organization, the Puerto Rican Fuerza Armadas Liberación Nacional, and others.[16] FBI assistant director of the Criminal Investigative Division Oliver "Buck" Revell outlined the model:

> We first experimented with the task force concept in 1979 when the bank robbery problem in New York City had grown to epidemic proportions. It became clear to the leadership of the New York City Police Department and the FBI that an innovative solution was required to address an increasingly dangerous situation. Accordingly, a formalized agreement, sealed by a signed memorandum of understanding, was entered into by both agencies. Detectives and FBI agents were detailed to a newly created task force housed in FBI space and jointly supervised by FBI and New York City Police Department personnel.

Among other things, this allowed the FBI to draw on the considerable resources of the local police, elements of which had not always been available to them.

One of the early members of what would come to be called the Joint Terrorist Task Force, Lieutenant Kevin Hallinan, described how things worked: "Police personnel assigned to the Terrorist Task Force must obtain a top-secret security clearance, in addition, to being sworn in as Special Deputy United States Marshall to facilitate their investigative needs while conducting terrorist investigations."[17] In this way, local police could be legally integrated into the federal apparatus. Law enforcement was evolving beyond what it had been in earlier periods.

In adopting this model, the agencies—officially anyways—were utilizing and adhering to new rules, and as such avoiding the politically detrimental pitfalls of carrying out what former FBI official W. Mark Felt called "extralegal" activities. According to Revell, "Task force investigative procedures conform to the requirements for Federal investigations and prosecutions . . . Federal policies and procedures. All aspects of every terrorism investigation are in accordance with the Attorney General's guidelines." This is a reference to the 1976 Levi Guidelines, which as we will see in the following chapter, required evidence of "specific and articulable facts" that a group was planning violence before an investigation could be initiated.[18]

Seen from the FBI's and other law enforcement's perspective, groups that had adopted political violence as a strategy coming off the sixties had unintentionally offered a laboratory for the FBI and local police to hone their investigative and repressive instruments. And this was happening at a time when the United States was undertaking a major shift in how it operated on the global stage.

## International Terrorism

These domestic measures played out amid a far more contentious international scene, one that saw more extreme acts of political terrorism than were happening in the United States.

In June 1979, soon-to-be secretary of state Alexander Haig, then the supreme commander of allied forces in Europe, was the target of an assassination attempt by Germany's Red Army Faction. Haig and his entourage were targeted by a remote-controlled bomb detonated under a small bridge in Belgium.[19] Haig and his driver narrowly escaped injury when the bomb exploded after their Mercedes

600 passed it, throwing the car into the air. Two months later, there was another terrorist attack. In this instance, the target was the former British military official, Earl Mountbatten of Burma. Mountbatten, who had been on holiday off the Irish Coast, was killed along with five family members and a crewman when a bomb planted by the Irish Republican Army (IRA) exploded.[20]

Such incidents were a harbinger of what was to come, with a far more international character—often embodying the contention between the United States and the Soviet Union, if the connections were not always transparent. Regardless, the curtain was being pulled closed on any lingering romance for political violence in the United States.

# 8

# The FBI, beyond Reform

---

> I don't say it's not legal, I say it's extralegal.
>
> —W. MARK FELT ON THE FBI'S ILLEGAL BREAK-INS, August 29, 1976

During the middle of the seventies, the FBI suffered a crisis of legitimacy as a result of its massive domestic intelligence program and the exposure of its Counterintelligence Program (COINTELPRO) that had targeted everyone from Dr. Martin Luther King to Hollywood actress Jean Seberg, with various and sundry dirty tricks, surveillance, and illegal break-ins.[1] By 1979, however, matters would turn away from exposure and accountability toward reasserting the power of the FBI and others in the law enforcement community.

## Deep Throat's Legacy

W. Mark Felt's remaining days on earth were few when he came out publicly in 2005 as "Deep Throat"—the informant who revealed Nixon's Watergate misdeeds. The identity of the informant, ostensibly secret, had been a topic of speculation for more than three decades. When he finally did come out, he was proclaimed "one of American democracy's heroes," though such plaudits were soon called into question.[2] The problem being that the man hailed for bringing down Nixon for his role in the illegal break-in at the Democratic National Headquarters was himself a convicted felon for, among other things, undertaking illegal break-ins in his capacity as an FBI official.[3]

The story of the pursuit of W. Mark Felt at the end of the seventies is a complicated one. On its surface, it suggests further accountability for FBI misdeeds. However, coming at a time when other priorities were rising for the U.S. political structure, the era of Bureau accountability was drawing to a close. In its place were efforts to re-energize the FBI and other agencies for the Cold War battles to come.

On August 22, 1976, the *New York Times* revealed that federal prosecutors were investigating the FBI for conducting a series of illegal break-ins and other measures aimed at the WU and other radical activists.[4] A week later, Felt, the former number-two man in the FBI, appeared on the national Sunday news show *Face the Nation* to unilaterally defend the agency: "Somebody has to come forward and stick up for the FBI. It's cheap to criticize the FBI now. And actually, the FBI is a wonderful organization. It's a magnificent organization filled with wonderful, wonderful people. And yet it is being attacked from every angle."[5] Felt also took the opportunity to (falsely) deny being the Nixon informant. As he told the panel of journalists, "I am not Deep Throat," though he added, "The only thing I can say is that I wouldn't be ashamed to be because I think whomever it was helped the country, no question about it."[6] It was a window into his practiced mendacity.

W. Mark Felt, aka "Deep Throat." Photo: U.S. Government.

In contrast to that dissembling, Felt openly admitted to things in another sphere, though in his mind it was simply part of doing his job. This was in regard to his organizing secret break-ins aimed at the WU and others. There, too, he misled his questioners when he was asked about break-ins against groups that were "not violence oriented." In response, Felt said, "I am unaware of those. I don't know about those. I've read about them in the paper too, but I was unaware of them in an official capacity."[7] His response was deliberately deceptive, something that would become clear when he was eventually put on trial.

The actions Felt revealed moved the Justice Department to act. On April 10, 1978, a federal grand jury handed down indictments against him and his colleague Edward S. Miller, as well as their former boss L. Patrick Gray—the acting director of the FBI after J. Edgar Hoover's death in 1972. The three were accused of conspiring to deprive American citizens of their civil rights. Over the course of the next two years, the case made its way through the courts.

While the indictments and pretrial activity merited a certain amount of media coverage, it was muted compared to the attention showered on the 1975 Church Committee. While that committee's revelations of the FBI's COINTELPRO initiatives against Martin Luther King, the Student Nonviolent Coordinating Committee, the BPP, and others were shocking, as extensive as they were they were far from comprehensive.[8] That was because even while they were underway, the FBI continued massive investigations on a number of left and radical organizations. Chief among these was the Communist Party USA (CPUSA)—the group that was the impetus for initiating COINTELPRO—accounting for almost 60 percent of all approved COINTELPRO operations.[9]

Put simply, amid the considerable—often staggering—revelations, there was a good deal the FBI did *not* make public. Not only was this because investigations were ongoing, but also because certain disclosures would have referenced "sources and methods" the Bureau needed to keep secret.[10] Among them was Operation SOLO, the name given to the highly placed informant within the CPUSA, Morris Childs, someone trusted to such a degree within the Party that he routinely met with leaders of the Soviet Union.[11] Beyond that were the FBI's considerable efforts against the Maoist group the Revolutionary Union and its founder Leibel Bergman. That investigation is wholly absent from the Church report—despite it being among the largest domestic security undertakings then underway.[12]

The Revolutionary Union investigation is especially telling in the way it revealed hard evidence of Felt and his associate's illegal

activity. This is on clear display in the trial testimony of FBI special agent David Ryan, in charge of the Bureau's "Bergman Investigation." Ryan made clear that as an FBI supervisor Felt not only
knew of the surveillance on Bergman, he was also tasked, with the
approval of J. Edgar Hoover, with ensuring it was effective. Specifically, at one point he traveled to San Francisco to make sure everything was in order when Bergman moved and the FBI needed to
place a listening device—referred to as "sensitive coverage"—in
his new home.[13] At trial, when Ryan was shown the applicable
order and asked to affirm its contents, he responded, "Yes, it reads,
'It is recommended Mr. Felt travel to San Francisco for on-the-
scene discussions along the above lines.'" When then asked, "And
does Mr. Hoover have a comment on that document?" he replied,
"Mr. Hoover states in his handwriting, 'I concur.'"[14] Not only does
this make clear the hands-on role of Felt, it also counters his claim
that he was ignorant of measures taken against people not involved
in violent activity—Bergman was not being pursued for matters of
political violence.

It was not only the targeting of Bergman that crossed that line.
Within Felt's released FBI file are thirteen single-page memos
headlined "DO NOT FILE"—a heading developed to circum-
vent disclosure by keeping them out of the official file system.[15]
All these memos, addressed to Felt from Miller, contain redac-
tions, obscuring their full content. However, several offer key
information. For example, one shows the subject line "Al Fatah—
Internal Security-Middle East," while several others reference the
Weathermen. Another is referenced, "U.S.-China [Peoples]
Friendship Association," an organization established to improve
relations between the United States and China. It lays out a plan
to break into the group's office: "On April 16, 1973, REDACTED
of the San Francisco office requested authority to contact an
anonymous source at an office building on REDACTED.
He assured me that such could be accomplished with full security,
and I gave him authority to proceed."[16] According to Ryan, the

Bureau had in fact conducted a break-in. When asked about the purpose, he explained:

> Well, a very standard technique in trying to identify intelligence apparatuses is to develop the funding. And at the time, as I recall, there was information indicating there had been some funding, either directly or indirectly to the U.S.-China Friendship Association. In any instance, we hoped to develop funding. We also hope to identify some of the individuals who were associated with the U.S.-China Friendship Association in anticipation of we might be able to tie them in to other individuals with whom we either had a photograph or we had only a first name or we had limited identifying information.[17]

The association, like Bergman, was not engaged in violence—nor were the authorities building a criminal case against it. It was being spied on because the FBI and government it worked for did not trust them. Leaving aside whether they were justified in being suspicious of a group that supported Maoist China—at a time when that country was opening to the West—the group was operating within the law.

Such disclosures coincided with a process whereby the government established specific rules for domestic security investigations—rules that could shield it from the embarrassment and delegitimating effect of the unconstrained efforts the FBI had been engaged in. Along with this, it established a mechanism to facilitate surreptitious break-ins, making such intrusions unambiguously legal.

## Levi Guidelines and the Foreign Intelligence Surveillance Act

In April 1976, Jimmy Carter's attorney general Edward Levi set new rules for domestic security investigations. No longer was mere advocacy of violence sufficient for the FBI to initiate an investigation.

Instead, it could proceed only after establishing "specific and artic-ulable facts giving reason to believe that an individual or group is or may be engaged in activities which involve the use of force or vio-lence."[18] The FBI's subjective assessment of a threat would no lon-ger be enough to open an investigation; it would now need evidence of an individual's or group's violent plans and actions.

The result was dramatic. The Bureau went from having 21,414 open investigations in July 1973 to 4,868 in March 1976. By May 1978, then FBI director William Webster said that the Bureau was "practically out of the domestic security field."[19] While that may have been an overstatement, it nonetheless reflected a qualita-tive shift in orientation. Rather than open-ended investigations, the FBI was to target for prosecution those engaged in or imminently planning violence—political or otherwise. The caveat of course was that any group attempting to advance the interest of a foreign power would be scrutinized relentlessly. In that respect, the CPUSA, in particular, would remain a high-profile focus.[20]

As for illegal break-ins and the like, there would be new rules there as well. As mentioned, Felt was forthright in admitting to "black bag" jobs, arguing that they were needed to protect against forces dangerous to the United States. In hindsight, this stands as laying the basis for the FBI to acquire the legal power to carry such measures out. This comes through in an exchange between journal-ist Ronald J. Ostrow and Felt on *Face the Nation*:

OSTROW [Couldn't] you go up on [Capitol] Hill and testify and you say here's the danger, we've got to have more authority now, rather than police taking authority in their own hands?

FELT Well, I think you're right. I think there should be legislation, but I'm simply telling you this is what's going on over many years.[21]

Within two years of that exchange, there was such legislation. In 1978 Congress enacted the Foreign Intelligence Surveillance Act (FISA), which established a court called the Foreign Intelligence

Surveillance Court (FISC), whose sole purpose was to review requests for intrusive surveillance.

The court, consisting of eleven federal district court judges chosen by the Chief Justice of the United States, was shrouded in secrecy from the beginning. It held its hearings in "nonpublic sessions" at which the only parties present were a single judge and representatives from the government. Warrants brought before the court allowed for all manner of intrusion, from electronic surveillance, monitoring phone calls, and physical searches to combing through business records.[22] When submitting a case for surveillance, the government did not have to prove a crime was underway or even was about to happen. It only needed to show the "target of the surveillance is a foreign power or agent of a foreign power," or that a significant purpose of the surveillance was to garner information on foreign political organizations and groups said to be engaged in international terrorism.[23] Not surprisingly the FISC was more than accommodating. In 1979, of the 199 applications "made for orders and extensions" of surveillance, none were denied.[24]

## The Killing of Fred Hampton

In the predawn hours of December 4, 1969, fourteen Chicago Police Department (CPD) officers, claiming they were searching for illegal weapons, raided a first-floor apartment on Chicago's Monroe Street. Inside, nine members of the Illinois BPP were in various phases of sleep. While police claimed they were fired on, the fusillade of over ninety bullets hit only Black Panthers. Two of them, Fred Hampton the chairman of the Illinois Panthers, and Mark Clark who had organized the group's Peoria chapter, were fatally wounded. Initially, the raid was seen as a success for the police, epitomized by the picture of grinning cops carrying Hampton's body out of the apartment, which circulated widely in the press. However, the one-sided nature of the attack quickly gave rise to questions. In this, not only were the Chicago police under scrutiny, but questions arose about the role of the FBI, which had been keeping close tabs on the Chicago Panthers. What would later be discovered was that the Bureau had a well-placed informant within the group. That informant had passed along a floor plan of the apartment to the CPD to facilitate their raid.[25]

To the degree most people today know the story of Fred Hampton, it is through the 2021 film *Judas and the Black Messiah*, a fictionalized account of the incident. The film, while dramatically riveting, is in important ways factually dubious. This is made clear in the movie's opening when it has J. Edgar Hoover, portrayed by Martin Sheen, proclaiming the Black Panthers "the greatest single threat to our national security, more than the Chinese, even more than the Russians." In reality, Hoover never said such a thing, nor would he, given how the Bureau and the U.S. government viewed China and the Soviet Union at that phase of the Cold War. Considering the power of such a statement, however, it is worth exploring how a variation of it found its way to becoming common knowledge.

In July 1969, Hoover talked to the media about the Bureau's annual report where he highlighted the current threats as seen by the FBI. In turn, United Press International ran a short piece titled "J. Edgar Hoover: Panthers Greatest Threat to US Security." As the article reported, "The Black Panther Party represents the greatest threat among the black extremist groups to the internal security of the United States, FBI director J. Edgar Hoover said today. Hoover said in his fiscal 1969 annual report the increased activity of 'violence-prone black extremist groups' had put more investigative responsibilities on the FBI. 'Of these,' Hoover said, 'the Black Panther party, without question, represents the greatest threat to the internal security of the country.'"[26] Given the headline, one could be forgiven for thinking Hoover was saying the BPP was the greatest threat to the U.S, as a whole—and it is the case that story has been the basis for the claim that the group was the FBI's preeminent target, rather than one of many challenges the Bureau confronted, in that period.[27]

Roy Martin Mitchell FBI personnel file. Photo: U.S. Government.

This, unfortunately, has had the effect of obscuring other matters also worthy of attention. In that respect, two characters who intersected with the Chicago Panthers, but also others, are worth a deeper look—FBI informant William O'Neal and his handler, Roy Martin Mitchell. William O'Neal was recruited by the FBI in 1968 after he had been arrested by Chicago police. O'Neal had been caught driving a car he had stolen from an auto rental agency. Nineteen at the time, he told the arresting officer that he was an FBI agent and flashed a phony ID. The police, in turn, referred the matter to the FBI who dispatched Special Agent Roy Martin Mitchell to meet with him.[28] According to O'Neal, Mitchell told him: "'I know you did it, but it's no big thing.' He said, 'I'm sure we can work it out.' And, um, I think a few, few months passed before I heard from him again, and one day I got a call and he told me that it was payback time. He said that 'I want you to go and see if you can join the Black Panther Party, and if you can, give me a call.'"[29] O'Neal went on to infiltrate the Panthers, first becoming

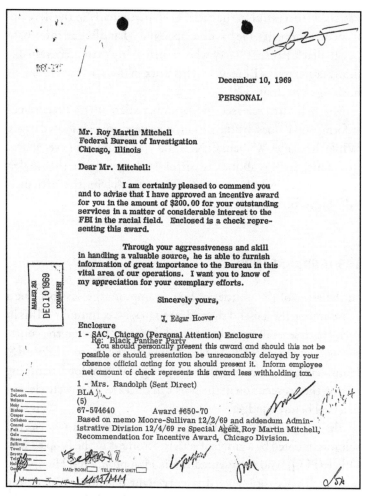

Memo from J. Edgar Hoover, Re: Roy M. Mitchell. Source: Mitchell FBI personnel file (U.S. Government).

the Chicago chapter's head of security and later chief of staff for Illinois.[30]

O'Neal's success within the BPP was intimately bound up with his work with his FBI handler. In the ranks of the FBI, Mitchell was considered an agent of impeccable quality, as this report from April 1969 affirms: "MITCHELL is a young Agent who has been

extremely successful in the racial field, particularly in the development of informants. He has developed and is handling an informant
in the Black Panther Party who is furnishing extremely valuable
information to the Bureau, and his work in this area has absolutely
nothing to be desired."[31]

Mitchell's file, released in December 2020 after a Freedom of
Information request by the author, runs nearly nine hundred pages.
While the names William O'Neal and Fred Hampton never appear
in the file, there is abundant corroborating evidence that makes
clear it was O'Neal who was the informant supplying the "extremely
valuable information."[32]

## The Hampton Trials

In the wake of the murder of Fred Hampton, the case became a
cause among the left and the wider progressive community. This in
turn led to several cases that wound their way through the courts
throughout the seventies. In 1972, Illinois state's attorney Edward S.
Hanrahan and twelve others were brought to trial for attempting
to stop the prosecution of the police in the case. They were cleared
in a trial before a judge.[33]

That, however, was not the end of their trouble. In 1970, a civil
suit was initiated by a group of activist attorneys in the People's Law
Office (PLO) who represented Iberia Hampton, Fred Hampton's
mother. That case involved twenty-eight defendants including
Hanrahan, three assistant state's attorneys, the Chicago police officers who conducted the raid, and the FBI's Marlin Johnson, Robert Piper, and Roy Martin Mitchell. The case went to trial in 1976
and lasted eighteen months. The judge, who was belligerent toward
the plaintiffs throughout, ended up throwing out the cases against
twenty-one of the defendants before the jury deliberated. The
remaining defendants had their charges dismissed when the jury
deadlocked on their cases. However, in April 1979 an appeals court
reversed the judge's decision and called for a new trial. In light of

that, the government settled the case, and the Hampton family was awarded $1.8 million in damages.[34]

In the course of the obstruction of justice trial and throughout the first few years of the civil suit, the identity of William O'Neal remained a closely held secret. However, developments in an unrelated 1973 case thrust him into the limelight.[35] In that year, Chicago police sergeant Stanley Robinson was arrested for the murder of twenty-two-year-old Jeff Beard. Robinson, as was revealed at trial, was the leader of a gang of corrupt Chicago cops who, among other things, carried out murder-for-hire. The government had built a solid case against Robinson and had established that in May 1972 he, with the help of another man, abducted Beard—under the pretense of arresting him—outside a Chicago pool hall. The two then drove the captive to Indiana where he was shot, stabbed, and beaten to death.[36]

Unfortunately for Robinson, his accomplice was also a government informant. His name was William O'Neal. While this meant a strong case for the government, for the Bureau and O'Neal it signaled the end of his role as a confidential informant. It also, when word came out in February 1973, alerted the attorneys in the PLO then pursuing the Hampton civil case that they needed to examine O'Neal's role in the Hampton killing. While they knew O'Neal had been Hampton's bodyguard, they had not known he was also working for the FBI.

With the revelation that O'Neal was an FBI informant, the PLO was able to push for disclosure in the course of their civil suit. One thing they learned was that the FBI had paid O'Neal a bonus of $300 for his work on the raid that killed Hampton. Not known at the time—that would take the release of Roy Mitchell's FBI file—was that Mitchell, too, had been paid a bonus, of $200. As J. Edgar Hoover noted in a commendation letter to Mitchell, "Through your aggressiveness and skill in handling a valuable source, he is able to furnish information of great importance to the Bureau in this vital area of our operations. I want you to know of my appreciation for your exemplary efforts."[37] While Hoover was careful not to spell out exactly what the "vital area of our operations" was, a notation at the bottom of the letter reads "Re: Black Panther Party." The timing, six days after Hampton's killing, makes clear what the award was for.

J. Edgar Hoover, however, would not be the only FBI director to commend Special Agent Mitchell for a killing in which his informant was a key player. In 1975, Eloise Beard, the sister of Jeff Beard, filed a lawsuit against Mitchell. The case argued that Mitchell had deprived her brother of his civil rights because of his "reckless training and use of an informant."[38] Mitchell, in other words, was culpable for Jeff Beard's death because of the way in which he had trained and handled William O'Neal. Mitchell, however, was ultimately not held to account. In August 1978, a court cleared him of any responsibility.

That ruling was cause for celebration in the U.S. Attorney's Office and the FBI. In a January 1979 letter from U.S. Attorney Thomas P. Sullivan to the director of the FBI, William Webster, Sullivan was effusive in his praise of Mitchell: "In October of this year, this office had the privilege of defending Special Agent Roy Martin Mitchell in a case in which Mr. Mitchell was alleged to have failed to supervise and train an informant being utilized by Mr. Mitchell and the F.B.I. As you are aware, after a three-week trial, the jury deliberated for approximately forty minutes and returned a verdict favorable to Mr. Mitchell. We perceive that verdict to be a total vindication of Mr. Mitchell's actions and the F.B.I.'s authorization of informants."[39] The prosecutor continued: "Mr. Mitchell is a man of the highest character, impeccable integrity, and a model F.B.I. agent whose attitude and activities should serve as a model for all Special Agents to emulate." Webster duly passed along the praise to the special agent—while the court decision clearing him essentially upheld an informant participating in murder.[40]

While the FBI and government attorneys would praise Mitchell, some in the CPD appear to have been less enamored. In a scene that might have been written for a television police procedural, a

United States Department of Justice

**UNITED STATES ATTORNEY**
NORTHERN DISTRICT OF ILLINOIS
UNITED STATES COURTHOUSE
CHICAGO, ILLINOIS 60604
WAB:cjh
January 8, 1979

William H. Webster, Director
Federal Bureau of Investigation
Washington, D. C. 20535

Re: Roy Martin Mitchell

Dear Mr. Webster:

In October of this year, this office had the privilege of defending Special Agent Roy Martin Mitchell in a case in which Mr. Mitchell was alleged to have failed to supervise and train an informant being utilized by Mr. Mitchell and the F.B.I. As you are aware, after a three week trial, the jury deliberated approximately forty minutes and returned a verdict favorable to Mr. Mitchell. We perceive that verdict to be a total vindication of Mr. Mitchell's actions and the F.B.I.'s authorization of informants.

In representing Mr. Mitchell, Assistant United States Attorneys experienced innumerable hours going over documents and working in close conjunction with Special Agent Mitchell. That experience was one of the most worthwhile and beneficial experiences those Assistant United States Attorneys will experience. Working with Mr. Mitchell was indeed a pleasure since Mr. Mitchell is a man of the highest character, impeccable integrity, and a model F.B.I. agent whose attitude and activities should serve as a model for all Special Agents to emulate. In reviewing Mr. Mitchell's career with the F.B.I., we are impressed by his dedication, public service, and high professional standards. In Special Agent Mitchell the F.B.I. and the citizens of this country have a precious commodity.

We will always cherish our participation in this case and look forward to the continuing friendship of Special Agent Mitchell and the Federal Bureau of Investigation.

Sincerely,

THOMAS P. SULLIVAN
United States Attorney

Assistant United States Attorney

Assistant United States Attorney

WILLIAM F. CONLON
Chief, Civil Division

U.S. Attorney General Thomas P. Sullivan's letter commending Roy M. Mitchell. Source: Mitchell FBI personnel file (U.S. Government).

report in Mitchell's personnel file recounts his harassment at the time of the Stanley Robinson case.

Specifically, there is a report on an April 1973 "apparently unwarranted arrest"—two months before the start of the Robinson trial—of Mitchell by a Chicago police officer for "driving an unsafe vehicle and for driving while under the influence." Mitchell, who is said to have had a flat tire after leaving a dinner with an assistant U.S. attorney, was confronted by a Chicago police officer who demanded that Mitchell, who was not drunk, take a breathalyzer test. When he refused, he was arrested.[41] As an FBI account of its investigation of the incident reports: "5 other Agents [were interviewed] who were engaged in an investigative assignment with him on the day in question. An AUSA [assistant U.S. attorney] who had dinner with SA Mitchell that evening was also interviewed. There is no indication whatsoever that SA Mitchell's version of the incident was other than factual."[42] The FBI then took the case to the CPD hierarchy. As a result, "the Commander, Chief of Detectives, and First Deputy Superintendent, Chicago Police Department (CPD), all apologized: and expressed regret over the arrest of SA Mitchell and advised that immediate steps would be taken to see that no further harassment was taken against him." It also reported that "the arresting officer would be admonished for his action on this particular occasion."[43]

In an effort to de-escalate the incident, the report says that "the best way to handle this current situation in order to avoid allegations of 'cover-up' would be to let SA Mitchell appear in court and explain his story to the judge." He was subsequently cleared in court of the DUI, but because of the flat tire he was made to pay a $25 fine for "driving an unsafe vehicle."[44]

While the episode was resolved amicably, it highlights how relations between the FBI and CPD were not without contention, and that neither was fully subservient to the other. This dispels a certain monolithic view often ascribed to the Bureau in its relations with the CPD, including, it would seem, in regard to the Hampton case.

## Mitchell and O'Neal's Complicity

The FBI's connection to the Hampton killing continues to carry a certain ambiguity—did they know the Chicago police were out to kill Hampton, or were they just happy to pass along information that would aid them in whatever suppressive plans they might undertake? True, they were pleased with the outcome, rewarding O'Neal and Special Agent Mitchell. Less clear, however, is O'Neal's specific role—substantial as it is—beyond passing along the floor plan.

The Jeff Beard case, however, is less ambiguous on O'Neal's participation. He drove to Indiana while Stanley Robinson guarded Beard in the car's back seat; he kept watch over Beard when Robinson stopped to make a phone call; and he "helped throw Beard's body over a fence" once he was dead.[45] In short, his role in facilitating the murder was essential. This was the basis for not one but two lawsuits: one against Mitchell, which was quickly decided against the plaintiff, and the other against O'Neal, which garnered a similar outcome.[46]

In making a final decision on the lawsuit brought against O'Neal, an appeals court cleared him of all responsibility, finding that "the issue, in this case, is whether that informant breached a constitutional duty owed to the murder victim and consequently caused the victim's death. We conclude, based on the undisputed facts, that he did not and thus we affirm the judgment of the district court."[47] Put simply, an informant had no obligation to stop a murder; indeed, they could facilitate such, so long as it was in the interest of building a criminal case. Given the essential nature of the use of informants, this was a strong affirmation of the use of one of the most unscrupulous methods by the FBI and like-minded law enforcement agencies.

The failure to find William O'Neal or Roy Mitchell as having any responsibility for the Jeff Beard murder and the killing of Fred Hampton was part of a larger process playing out in the last years of the seventies. Not only was there the legitimation of domestic spying offered by the Levi Guidelines and the establishment of the FISC, but a reaffirmation of the role of the FBI.

W. Mark Felt and Edward S. Miller would not go to trial until 1980, and though they were convicted, the judge imposed nothing more than a $5,000 fine. Even that was quickly put aside. In April 1981, Ronald Reagan pardoned the pair, writing: "America was at war in 1972, and Messrs. Felt and Miller followed procedures they believed essential to keep the Director of the FBI, the Attorney General, and the President of the United States advised of the activities of hostile foreign powers and their collaborators in this country."[48] The days of looking into the darker aspects of the FBI and holding it to account, as tenuous as they were, were over.

# 9

# After Disco

Our message was more urgent—that things were going to pieces.

**—MICK JONES ON THE MAKING OF**
***LONDON CALLING*, 2013**

They billed it as a "Disco Demolition." On July 12, 1979, during the interval of a baseball doubleheader between the Chicago White Sox and the Detroit Tigers, WLUP DJ Steve Dahl promised to blow up disco records on the playing field. Everyone was invited to Comiskey Park to witness the event. To encourage a big crowd, admission was reduced to 98 cents. The gimmick worked. The stadium filled with fifty thousand people, with another fifteen thousand kept out but refusing to leave. According to one guard, "We were trying to hold the main gate closed, but the kids forced it open. The ushers got beat up. We just couldn't control them." Many of those who showed up had brought their own records to add to the pyre—security was too overwhelmed to confiscate them. When the big moment came, the explosion went off as planned.

However, rather than being the culmination, it served as a starter pistol. Fans began tossing their vinyl disco records they had brought to the stadium like frisbees. They then descended onto the field en masse. There were too many for those charged with security to hold them back. The authorities were so beleaguered that the mostly teenage crowd held the field uncontested. When the cops did arrive, it took them a half hour—wielding clubs—to regain control.[1]

Dahl, the provocateur behind the event, attempted to rationalize the disorder: "If the Sox had won the pennant and the fans stormed the field, the headlines in the newspapers would have read: 'Baseball fans overzealous.' But because the incident is associated with rock 'n roll, they call it a riot, and all the old ladies in Tinley Park phone Wally Phillips [a Chicago radio personality] and say, 'Isn't it Terrible?'"[2] This was not, however, a pennant victory—as out of control as such things can be. This was a riot with an ugly subtext. Dave Marsh writing in *Rolling Stone* observed, "White males, eighteen to thirty-four, are the most likely to see disco as the product of homosexuals, blacks and Latins, and therefore they're most likely to respond to appeals to wipe out such threats to their security. It goes almost without saying that such appeals are racist and sexist, but broadcasting has never been an especially civil-libertarian medium."[3] Marsh's comments, if a bit overbroad, were mainly on point.

Disco, like any form of pop music, ran a gamut. While there was a goodly amount of it that was self-focused, commodity-promoting, and hedonistic—and its ubiquity for a few years in the seventies was overwhelming—like most musical forms it cut two ways. As one columnist noted, "Disco is, in a sense, rebellion, too, but disco's rebellion is not against society but against the growing excesses of rock; disco's simplicity versus rock's growing artistic pretensions."[4] It was also for its time, on the cutting edge musically, at times revelatory and innovative. None of this, however, was up for debate at Comiskey Park. The verdict was encompassed in a small-minded slogan: "Disco sucks."

The mob action in Chicago—disordered and contradictory as it was—was one of several cultural manifestations as the seventies drew to a close. These ranged from horrifying to transcendent, but taken in aggregate they suggested events were headed far beyond the heretofore complacency that was the seventies state of things.

## The Who in Cincinnati

The youth who took the field in Chicago were a prototype for audiences who turned out for the big stadium shows that had become the staple of rock in the seventies. Much of the most popular rock music had traveled a fair distance away from the experimentation and embrace of other forms of the previous decade. In its place were mega-attractions heavy on power chords and performance gimmicks, such as Ted Nugent, KISS, Peter Frampton, and Led Zeppelin. While these performers had differing degrees of artistry, what they held in common was they were the centerpiece in the money-making juggernaut set loose by those promoting their concerts.

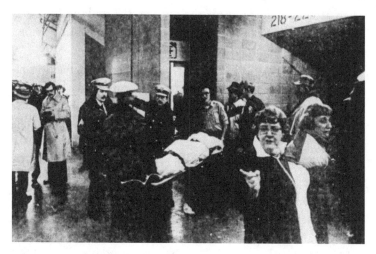

Outside Riverfront Stadium, December 1979. Photo: Karl Kuntz, *Cincinnati Post*, December 4, 1979.

Among the top bands in this category were the Who. Unlike a good many of their peers, the group had successfully transitioned from the counterculture sensibilities of the sixties to become a major money-making draw in the seventies. However, when the group set out to tour in 1979, they were still recovering from the loss of their drummer Keith Moon a year earlier. As such, the tour—split between Europe and the United States—was to be their renaissance. This was the backdrop to their show on December 3 in Cincinnati at the thirteen-thousand-seat Riverfront Stadium.

There was a great deal of anticipation for the group's show in Ohio. Fans had started lining up for the evening performance at 1:30 P.M., knowing that being at the head of the line in a general admission concert was the best shot at getting a good spot for the show. However, when the venue did start letting people in, all the doors did not open. What ensued was a frenzy to get at good seats combined with the panic of being in a crowd crush where there was no safe exit. This led to chaos in which people fell and could not regain their footing. As a result, people were trampled by a crowd so tight that even those wanting to help could not. A testament to the gruesomeness of the scene was the fact that when attendees finally made their way to the stadium floor and began filling up the open area in front of the stage, some among them noticed blood on their shoes.

For their part, the Who went on as scheduled, making no mention of the tragedy. This was not out of callousness but in the interests of not further aggravating things that an acknowl- edgment could trigger. In the end, seven young men and four young women died.

The incident was horrible, made worse by its portrayal in the media, which was quick to lay blame for the tragedy on the audi- ence. The *Guardian*, which headlined its report "Drugs a Cause of Panic Which Killed Who Fans," reported that "some of those out- side were already high on cheap wine, 'downers,' pot, or the latest fashionable drug among American teenagers, PCP or 'angel dust,' which is a tranquilizer for horses."[5] Cincinnati's mayor J. Kenneth

Blackwell, while laying the blame on festival seating, also took a shot at the concertgoers: "A lot of young people apparently had been out there a long time before the doors opened. They were cold. Some were drinking alcohol. Some were smoking marijuana, and when the doors opened, all sense of rationality left the group."[6]

For its part, the *New York Times* saw fit to draw a connection to the "most notorious rock concert": Altamont in 1969. Altamont, however, unlike the show in Cincinnati, was a free event with a much larger crowd—attended by three hundred thousand. And while it was the site of tragedy, there were only three deaths, two of which were accidental, the other a fatal encounter between knife-wielding Hells Angels and a young Black man with a pistol.[7]

By contrast, the far smaller concert in Cincinnati saw not only many more fatalities but systemic disregard by authorities for the youth. As one of the concertgoers, whose friend was hospitalized, described the situation, "There were policemen out front not doing anything, looking through the door. They saw people being crushed to death right in front of them. . . . It was just like being treated like cattle. They had all their money, the only thing to worry about was gate-crashers."[8]

The horror in Ohio underscored just how commodified the rock audience had become. Rather than human beings, they were seen by promoters and stadium owners as nothing more than ticket holders—a view that informed things going forward.

## Bruce Springsteen

In contrast to events in Chicago and Cincinnati, Brue Springsteen by the end of the decade was ascending as a rock artist who not only had a unique bond with his audience but was someone who had something urgent to say about life in the country he inhabited.

Springsteen had broken into the mainstream in 1975 with his valentine to youthful working-class rebelliousness, *Born to Run*. In the aftermath of that album, however, he was sidelined for almost a year due to a suit and countersuit with his former manager Mike Appel. Putting that behind him, he released what some consider his best album, 1978's *Darkness on the Edge of Town*.[9]

Between the two albums, something had shifted in Springsteen's outlook and was reflected in his songwriting. Where *Born to Run* held the promise of getting to a place "where we can walk in the sun," *Darkness* offered only the solace of washing up after work to go "racing in the street"—a bleak callback to the exuberance of Martha and the Vandellas' "Dancing in the Street." Whatever Springsteen's impetus, the songs captured the mood of downscaled dreams and the disenchantment of a section of the population, especially youth. While the full degree of transformation that lay ahead for the working class was outside anyone's purview, there was a palpable sense that the way of life that had been in place was disappearing and what lay outside those boundaries was not pretty.

Whether taking the form of boisterous rock 'n' roll or a shout of rage, Springsteen's new direction resonated. In concert, he could count on his audience, which was filling larger and larger venues, to sing out the appropriate lyric if he went silent during a verse. This was a mutually reinforcing relationship. Music critic Robert Hilburn described how this worked at one 1978 show in Los Angeles:

> When he jumps from the stage into the audience, it's not just a token gesture. He sometimes races up and down the various aisles and even up 10 to 12 steps of the side loges. When Forum security guards got between him and the audience, he challenged them. "Hey, you two guys work here or something?" He asked when guards pushed fans back during one of his ventures into the audience. "These people are just my friends." At another point. Springsteen leaped from the stage to lead an aisle full of fans past a guard blockade to the edge of the stage.[10]

For his record company, establishment media, and promoters, Springsteen checked all the boxes. He was a money-making machine who would be marketed for all he was worth. This was facilitated by the fact that—as good as he was as an artist—he was also rebellious, without being particularly radical. As such, he could speak to a wide audience. All that allowed him to stand as a phenomenon, emblematic of changes in the works. As he would later sing, America was headed to a not-good place on a "Down-bound Train."

## Born Again Dylan

Where Springsteen offered something akin to a secular revival, Bob Dylan exited the decade offering a religious one.

Dylan had begun the seventies with suggestions of embracing his previous political bent. This included a song on the killing of Black revolutionary George Jackson and a performance of some of his most topical songs at the benefit concert for Bangladesh organized by his friend George Harrison. Mid-decade he undertook the Rolling Thunder Review, which included everyone from Joan Baez to Roger McGuinn, where he performed some of his best songs in his original voice. During this time, he co-wrote the song "Hurricane," a defense of the jailed African American boxer Ruben "Hurricane" Carter. Carter's case, like that of George Jackson, ended up as more complicated than Dylan's songs suggested, but these songs signaled that Dylan was, at least to a degree, ready to re-enter the political fray.[11]

Any notion, however, that he would continue to dabble in matters of secular social justice was put aside when he came out as a born-again Christian. Notably, Dylan's conversion was not super-ficial. As he said, "I asked lots of questions, questions like, 'What's the son of God, what's all that mean?' and 'What does it mean—dying for my sins?'" In obtaining answers to those questions from those around him—artists who considered themselves born again—Dylan concluded that "Jesus was real." As he said, "I wanted that. . . . I knew that He wasn't going to come into my life and make it miserable, so one thing led to another until I had this feeling, this vision, and feeling."[12] His conversion, in other words, was hardcore.

While Dylan was entitled to believe whatever he wished, such beliefs had resonance far beyond him personally. As such, pushback ensued. As one columnist pointed out, "Dylan once had the funky charisma to shape the attitudes of an entire generation. Now a lot of his old fans just cackle when he comes on with his born-again harangues."[13] The latter is a reference to Dylan's openly proselytizing during his concerts. Of course, anyone who listened closely to his earlier songs, such as "Shelter from the Storm" from 1975's *Blood on the Tracks*, might have surmised that Dylan might be inclined to steer clear of any maelstroms the upcoming decade might throw up. Nonetheless, it was a shock and disappointment for many longtime fans.

Despite all this, his conversion had contradictory elements. On the one hand, he was preaching a doctrine with little room for compromise. The song "Change My Way of Thinking" is exemplary. It contains the lyric "He who is not for Me is against Me" from Matthew 12:30—a passage that bears no small similarity to Eldridge Cleaver's famous maxim "You either have to be part of the solution, or you're going to be part of the problem."[14] Dylan's Christianity, in other words, was a scolding and uncompromising one.[15] At the same time, he did not hitch his conversion to the arising right-wing evangelical movement. When asked about this specifically, he responded, "I think people have to be careful about all that. . . . It's real dangerous. You can find anything you want in the Bible. You can twist it around any way you want, and a lot of people do that. I just don't think you can legislate morality."[16]

Regardless of such nuance—and to the consternation of no small number of his millions of fans—his conversion effectively removed him from the worldly public stage at this pivotal moment. It would be well into the 1980s before he returned to being a secular artist.

## Rumblings in the United Kingdom

Like the United States, the United Kingdom was undergoing a period of economic transformation and disruption. Amid this was the rise of a racist anti-immigrant movement embodied in the ultra-right National Front. Notably, this movement would generate contention within the musical sphere.

On the negative end was rock icon Eric Clapton. By mid-decade, Clapton, who had battled heroin addiction and alcoholism, went on record supporting the National Front. This was on full display during an extended rant at a 1976 concert where he complained about "wogs and coons"—"wogs" being British slang for non-white people. He also infamously embraced the xenophobia of Enoch Powell, a right-wing politician famous for his anti-immigrant views. Powell was notable for what came to be called the "Rivers of Blood" speech that railed against immigration. Troublingly, Clapton called Powell "a prophet."[17]

Another rock star, this one ascendant in comparison to Clapton, whose best work was already behind him, was David Bowie.[18] While Bowie did not make racist and anti-immigrant statements, he did declare his admiration for fascism. Specifically, in a 1976 *Playboy* interview with music journalist Cameron Crowe, Bowie said, "I believe very strongly in fascism." He then compared it to a rock concert: "People aren't very bright, you know. They say they want freedom, but when they get the chance, they pass up Nietzsche and choose Hitler, because he would march into a room to speak and music and lights would come on at strategic moments. It was rather like a rock 'n' roll concert. The kids would get very excited—girls got hot and sweaty and guys wished it was them up there. That, for me, is the rock 'n' roll experience."[19] The statement, as contemptuous of his audience as it was, seemed more intended to shock than to promote a philosophy, and he would later renounce it. It was, nonetheless, problematic.

Whatever their thinking, Clapton's and Bowie's statements came amid a contentious situation in which younger artists were pushing back against these and other racist and fascist manifesta-tions. The most overt expression of this came via the Rock Against Racism (RAR) movement.

RAR sought to challenge the National Front and the ideology behind it. To that end, there were several high-profile concerts and carnivals that attracted some of the best artists of their day, most of whom were in the early phase of their success. This included groups such as the English Beat, the Specials, the Tom Robinson Band, and Graham Parker and the Rumour.[20] Of these, one group especially stood out.

## The Clash's Moment

Writing in the *Los Angeles Times*, pop music critic Robert Hilburn described Clash lead singer Joe Strummer like this: "He sings . . . with the anxious expression of a man whose car has just stalled in the path of a speeding train."[21] Driving Strummer and the band's urgency was a connection to the contemporary political scene.

In 1979, the group embarked on their first tour of the United States to promote their second album, *Give 'Em Enough Rope*.

The Clash, 1980. Photo: Helge Øverås.

Fortuitously, they found themselves in America during the flurry of events of that year: the Three Mile Island (TMI) meltdown, the Iranian Revolution, the invasion of Afghanistan, and much else. All of this would, in ways obvious and subtle, inform their third, and breakout, album, *London Calling*.

That record, a modest success at the time, is today heralded as one of the best records of the rock era.[22] What set it apart was not simply its musical energy—ranging in genre from rock to R&B to jazz to reggae—but the degree to which it captured the intensity of the moment.

Some of the selections were simply passionate reworkings. Songs such as "Brand New Cadillac" was a cover of the 1959 rockabilly hit by Vince Taylor. Similarly, "Wrong 'Em Boyo," was a cover of the Jamaican ska band the Rulers' take on the legendary "Stagger Lee." Other songs, however, traversed uncharted territory. "Spanish Bombs" was a concatenation of themes: the Spanish Civil War, the murdered poet Garcia Lorca, and the contemporary struggles in Northern Ireland and the Basque region of Spain, all recounted by a narrator flying on a DC-10 jet—a reference to two DC-10 crashes in 1979, one in May in Chicago that killed 243, the other in Mexico City in October that killed 77.[23] Those incidents, coming on the heels of TMI, were seen as another ominous herald, much like the album's title song, "London Calling," with its allusion to TMI and the meltdown expected. As Mick Jones explained, "A headline on the front of the London Evening Standard [warned] that the North Sea might rise and push up the Thames, flooding the city. We flipped. To us, the headline was just another example of how everything was coming undone."[24] In a similar vein, the song "Clampdown" told of one or two dictators—the Iranian Shah and Nicaragua's Somoza—paying their due. That song was followed by "Guns of Brixton," a contemporary urban folk tale of meeting the hostility of police with your finger on the trigger of your own gun.

This was beyond anything punk, as pathbreaking as it could be, or any other music was tackling at the time. While the album did not make its way into major circulation until the following year, it nonetheless served as an artistic document, birthed amid, and memorializing the tumult of, 1979.

## Reggae

The Clash were among a number of bands to emerge from the British punk and new wave movement who drew on an appreciation—sometimes appropriation—of reggae music.

Reggae had gained a certain following in the seventies—more so in the United Kingdom than the United States, the former having a large West Indian population.[25] The music was remarkable in large part for its rebellious, if largely pan-Africanist, content, albeit shrouded in the precepts of the Rastafarian religion. Among the beliefs of Rastafarianism is that the Ethiopian dictator Haile Salisse is God, based on the Jamaican Marcus Garvey's vision: "Look to Africa where a black king shall be crowned, he shall be the Redeemer."[26] Beyond its religious tenets, however, was a fiercely rebellious sensibility.

In the seventies, among the foremost figures of the genre were Peter Tosh, Bob Marley, and Jimmy Cliff. Cliff had become famous via his starring role in the 1972 film *The Harder They Come*. Marley and Tosh, along with Bunny Wailer, broke through with the group the Wailers. However, by the mid-seventies, the three had struck out on their own. The most successful in this regard were Marley and Tosh.

If not the most politically radical, Tosh was the most militant of the trio. As one profile noted, "Peter Tosh is a flamboyantly angry man, and his music of the last decade reflects this, the singer roaring in his sulfurous baritone about racial injustice, police brutality, exploitation of the poor, general inequity and the fire and brimstone finale that awaits this sinful planet."[27] This was on sharp display on his 1977 album *Equal Rights*, which reprised the Wailers' rebellious anthem "Get Up, Stand Up" and included the millenarian "Downpressor Man." However, 1979's *Mystic Man* was tilted more toward Tosh's religious outlook, and as such was less accessible to a larger audience. Musically, too, Tosh had a harder sound, which limited his appeal to a degree.

By contrast, Bob Marley was a more approachable vehicle to popularize reggae. As one columnist put it, Marley as reggae's "angry young man . . . stands with Jackson Browne and Bruce Springsteen as one of this decade's indispensable rock artists."[28] In 1978, he released *Kaya*, which contained a good number of love songs, suggesting a toning down of more edgy matters. However, the times being what they were, he followed that with 1979's *Survival*, which the *Los Angeles Times* called "his most forceful in years."[29] Among its most radical songs, "Babylon System" referred to the dominant means of rule people were living under in Africa and Marely's Jamaica as being akin to a vampire "sucking the blood of the sufferers." And this on an album whose cover shows a historical schematic of a packed slave ship. Among the album's songs was a paean to the imminent independence of "Zimbabwe." All of which is testimony to the impact the times were having on Marley's—and others'—music.

On the whole, it was amid these various incidents, upheavals, and explorations that the cultural landscape was shifting. The escapist hold of disco and elements of hard rock were giving rise to new, and sometimes radical, musical expressions. While they would abate as the new decade got fully underway, for the moment they burned with a brilliant incandescence.

# 10

# Morality Wars

Freedom can therefore never be
construed without relation to the
truth as revealed by Jesus Christ,
and proposed by his Church, nor
can it be seen as a pretext for
moral anarchy.

—**JOHN PAUL II**, Philadelphia,
October 3, 1979

On August 28, 1978, the Catholic world celebrated as Albino
Luciani was officially elevated to the papacy, becoming Pope John
Paul I, replacing Paul VI, who had died earlier that month. Thirty-
three days later, John Paul himself succumbed—apparently of a
heart attack—once again leaving empty the Throne of Saint Peter.
World Catholicism was not having an easy time of it at the end of
the seventies.

The church's transition, however, did get resolved, when the College of Cardinals anointed Karol Wojtyła Pope John Paul II, a

decision that would have a profound impact in the ensuing decade. Wojtyła's reign, while a popular one, would nonetheless be stamped with his reactionary views on social and political matters.

His thinking was clear from the beginning, especially regarding communism. As Zbigniew Gorecki, editor of a Polish religious newspaper in Chicago opined, "He has had a great deal of experience with communism, he knows the tactics of communism and its relation to religion." Similarly, Bishop John Ward, the auxiliary of the Los Angeles Diocese, said, "The leaders in Communist-controlled Poland are going to have to take a second look at this man.... He was a religious leader in their midst; now he is rocketed into the supreme leadership of Roman Catholics around the world. He never seemed awed by the opposition. He was fearless in speaking out for human rights." Jimmy Carter's geopolitical czar Zbigniew Brzezinski was similarly enthusiastic: "He will make a great Pope.... [He] is a man who understands the reality of the modern world."[1]

Wojtyła's thinking in this regard was most pronounced in his hostility to liberation theology—a school of thought gaining popularity among the impoverished and disregarded in Central and South America. In the pope's view, liberation theology was a deviation "damaging to the faith and to Christian living."[2]

The new pope's reactionary views were not just confined to anti-communism, but included his views on abortion and sexuality: "In today's society, we see so many disturbing tendencies and so much laxity regarding the Christian view on sexuality that have all one thing in common: recourse to the concept of freedom to justify any behavior that is no longer consonant with the true moral order and the teaching of the Church."[3] Put another way, there was traditional morality—sex between a man and woman for procreation—and there was this new morality that was an abomination in the face of God.

All of this was seen as useful, and a positive development for those who would come to occupy the key positions of political and military power in the United States as they shifted toward a final Cold War confrontation with the Soviet Union. The new pope's views also meshed well with an energized right wing, one moving deliberately into the realm of U.S. electoral politics.

## The Christian Right

While the pope operated on the international stage, domestically another type of moral conservatism was positioning itself to play a forceful role. This was the Christian right, which had at its core three abiding principles: anti-abortion—meaning fundamental opposition to women's equality and freedom—anti–gay rights, and anti-communism. All of these positions were couched in the rhetoric of family values and against moral decay.

The rise of this movement coincided with the convulsions of the sixties that had sharply challenged conventional religion. For those who had not forgone religion entirely, there were efforts to draw them in—abandoning conventional rituals such as sitting quietly in the pew on Sunday and adopting more popular methods. That included such things as *The Living Bible*—which also came in an illustrated version called *The Way*—a popular reworking of the original, along with adopting a more communal vibe, replete with guitars and group singing.[4] Along with this were popularizations on Broadway, with productions like *Godspell, Jesus Christ Superstar*, and *Joseph and the Amazing Technicolor Dream Coat*. Such things, and others, were aimed at bringing the alienated back into the fold.[5]

By the late 1970s, however, the Christian right had integrated some of these elements to make themselves more appealing. This included the development of "mega-churches," where services came to resemble rock concerts with abundant communal singing rather than staid rituals.[6] Despite such progressive trappings, at the core of many of these new or transformed churches lay reactionary politics.

## Christian Broadcasting

Hand in hand with the advent of modern mega-churches was the proliferation and expansion of Christian mass media via television and radio. A report in the *Los Angeles Times* in January 1979 noted that for "the past three years, new Christian radio stations in the United States have been going on the air at a rate of one a week." In the even more influential medium of television, there were said to be thirty-five active Christian stations, with applications pending with the Federal Communications System for twenty more.[7]

Among the heavies at the center of this movement was Jerry Falwell and his "Old Time Gospel Hour," which broadcast out of Virginia. Falwell was a political reactionary of the first order, and would come to be called a "cultural warrior." Little surprise, then, that he also supported the conservatism of the new pope. In his view, the pope's "uncompromising stand against abortion and homosexuality and for the monogamous family set a healthy tone for all of us."[8] A further sense of his reactionary disposition came in 1978 when he visited Southern California to advocate for something called "Proposition 6," a measure that would allow gay and lesbian teachers to be fired if it was shown that they had "engaged in homosexual activity."[9] While that measure was defeated, it was a skirmish in a more long-term war.

But Falwell was not simply a cultural warrior—he also held to a hardcore Cold War stance. One newspaper feature on him noted that "he suggests repeatedly that a weak-willed United States might capitulate to an 'overwhelmingly' weapons-superior Soviet Union in the 1980s." Falwell, not surprisingly, would come to wield his not inconsequential political power to support like-minded politicians, thus bolstering the power of the right evangelical movement.

In this, Falwell was joined by similar-thinking evangelicals. There was Pat Robertson and his *The 700 Club*, a widely distributed television show. Robertson's influence would only increase over the coming years. And there was the Reverend Robert C. Grant. Grant, head of the Pasadena-based lobbying group Christian Voice, supported efforts against abortion and gay rights. Along with this, he opposed the SALT II treaty and supported the anti-communism of Taiwan against mainland China. In Grant's view, the United States is "the last stronghold of Christian faith on the planet, [and it] has come under increasing attack from Satan's forces in recent years."[10] While such thinking might be dismissed as comical, the fact that it resonated within the evangelical community meant it could not be easily dismissed.

It was not only men, however, incubating out of this movement. There were also the likes of Anita Bryant, a former Miss Oklahoma who had become an orange juice pitch-person with a national profile. Bryant emerged as a cultural warrior as far back as 1969 when she attended a Rally for Decency after the Doors' lead singer, Jim Morrison, was said to have exposed himself—a charge not proven—during a concert.[11] As the seventies proceeded, she became a vocal advocate opposing gay rights, albeit couched in the pseudo-Christian ethos of saving them: "I want to help them [homosexuals] to find the love of Jesus in their own hearts and return to God's moral law."[12] In 1977, Bryant launched a successful campaign against a Dade County ordinance that prohibited discrimination based on sexual orientation.[13] By 1979, she had become the go-to person for anti-gay statements, so when twenty-five thousand marched in Washington, DC, in October for gay rights, Bryant sent a telegram to the marchers letting them know she was praying "for those misguided individuals who seek to flaunt their immoral lifestyle."[14] The press duly publicized her response.

Less widely known at the time, but more strategically threatening long term, was Phyllis Schlafly. Schlafly, through her Eagle Forum, initially directed her anti–women's rights and traditional morality efforts against the then-pending Equal Rights Amendment (ERA). That measure, which sought to enshrine equality in the Constitution, was anathema to Schlafly and the strengthening

Anita Bryant, Save Our Children fundraising card, 1977. Source: Stonewall Library and Archives.

right. In her view, the "women libbers" who had emerged as a major force in the early seventies were losing ground, and she and her people were "the most powerful force in the country."

Along with such bravado, when convenient, these forces were happy to cast themselves as besieged underdogs. At the Eighth Annual Meeting of Schlafly's Eagle Forum, established to defeat the ERA, one of the attendees cast the issue in the terms of early Christianity: "Us and the NOW [National Organization for Women] people . . . it's like the Christians and the lions." Underneath the particulars of the stop-ERA initiative, however, was a strategy based on a 1950s sensibility of women having a subservient social role—a core tenet of this right-wing conservative movement.[15]

## Right and Wrong and Vietnam

While the religious right was sharpening its knives, another more insidious type of reaction was asserting itself, in regard to what the American public was being offered in relation to movies about the Vietnam War.

Vietnam, the only war the United States had ever lost, was an important and lingering problem for the country. When World War II ended, there was no shortage of movies memorializing that struggle. While they ranged from the more nuanced *Best Years of Our Lives* to the cartoonish, *Sands of Iwo Jima*, the war was nonetheless a bounty for national cultural cohesion and examples of moral rectitude. In Vietnam, however, such films were few and far between. John Wayne tried with *The Green Berets*, but it fell flat. The *New York Times* called that film "unspeakable" and "stupid," and "an invitation to grieve, not for our soldiers or for Vietnam (the film could not be falser or do a greater disservice to either of them) but for what has happened to the fantasy-making apparatus in this country."[16] As a clarion call to support the war, it moved only those already inclined to do so. For the larger ruling apparatus, it was an embarrassment.

After the war was lost, it became an even bigger challenge to assert something positive and patriotic about the Vietnam experience. On the one hand, Hollywood, for all its liberal pretensions, was fundamentally steeped in the chauvinist assumption that the U.S. model of democracy was the superior one in the world. Because of this, it was not going to challenge American pre-eminence in any fundamental way. However, given the debacle of Vietnam, saying as much without sufficient nuance was problematic. As such, Hollywood in the immediate years following the war said nary a thing. However, as the decade wore on, a number of films began to appear that made their points in more subtle ways.

In 1978 Jane Fonda and John Voight starred in *Coming Home*—a film revolving around the pain the war had inflicted on those sent to fight it. It was sympathetic to the plight of veterans, both pro- and anti-war. The film's culminating scene has the wheelchair-bound John Voight character, Luke, deliver a speech to highschoolers about his journey from wanting to "kill for my country" to a confession that he did things he "finds hard to live with." As he gives his speech, we see another character, played by Bruce Dern, who is also a returned veteran, ceremoniously remove his military uniform and then run naked into the Pacific Ocean to end his life. The film was a kind of catharsis—suffused with both sorrow and rage. It won the acceptance of the status quo, garnering Academy Awards for both Fonda and Voight.

That film, however, which walked the tightrope of indicting the war but not the warrior, was not especially helpful in reasserting something essential for the rulers of the United States—motivating its young people to be willing to fight and die for its global authority. Of course, brazen propaganda was not going to work—too much had happened for all but a hard core to be moved by that. For that, elements of ambiguity were needed. In that regard, Francis Ford Coppola's *Apocalypse Now* played an important role, regardless of whatever the larger intentions of the director.

Coppola's film proceeds as a fever dream traveling through the "Heart of Darkness"—the title of the Joseph Conrad novella on which the film is based—in this case, Vietnam. It is a savage and surreal place. At issue is Colonel Kurtz, who has "gone rogue" and is operating outside the official command structure. As such, in the military's euphemistic terminology, he needed to be terminated. The film is replete with moral ambiguity. We even get "comedy" in the form of (the unsubtly named) Colonel Kilgore. The colonel as we are shown can be both tender—ensuring a young Vietnamese child and mother are sent to a hospital—and absurdly ruthless: in calling in a napalm strike he says he "loves the smell of napalm in the morning." It is all surreal, and intentionally so, but cutting through the artistic gauze is a film that portrays the Vietnamese, at best, as little more than props, while U.S. soldiers are drawn with an underlying—if conflicted—humanity.

*Apocalypse Now* was lauded as one of the best war movies ever made, an assessment largely made by those comfortably living in the United States. Roger Ebert—who loved the film—nonetheless understood its inherent myopia. As he recalled, "Once at the Hawaii Film Festival, I saw five North Vietnamese films about the war—they never mentioned 'America,' only 'the enemy,' and one director told me, 'It is all the same—we have been invaded by China, France, the U.S.'"[17] It was a deflating assessment of the American view that held the U.S. defeat in Vietnam as something extraordinary and unique, if not incomprehensible.

Where *Apocalypse Now* contained different shades of gray, *The Deer Hunter* was less ambiguous. As such, it found wide approval in the critical press and film community. On its release, it was lauded. Gene Siskel, with oblivious condescension, praised the film: "It's hard to imagine a more loving tribute to 'good, working class people.'"[18] *New York Times* critic Vincent Canby cast a more conflicted eye: "Not once does anyone question the war or his participation in it." He went on to ask, "What are these veterans left with? Feelings of contained befuddlement, a desire to make do and, perhaps, a more profound appreciation for love, friendship, and community."[19] The latter comment is an allusion to the concluding scene where the returned vets and their partners sing an at first tenuous then full-on rendition of "God Bless America" as they prepare to eat. It is a moving scene, shot through with ambiguity, but one that suggests the best way to get through all the pain is to hold tight to one another *and* to one's country. *The Deer Hunter* would win the Academy Award for Best Picture in 1979.

## The White Night Riot

While such undertakings—at times conscious, others simply systemic—worked to reaffirm traditional morality or revanchist patriotism, they did so in a situation in which the genie was largely out of the bottle. This was particularly true in the matter of gay rights, which was on sharp display on May 20, 1979, when a jury in San Francisco returned a verdict against Dan White.

White was the former San Francisco supervisor who had gone to the city hall offices of Mayor George Moscone and Supervisor Harvey Milk—the city's first openly elected gay politician—and shot both of the men dead in cold blood. White, who had been put on trial for first-degree murder—refused to take responsibility for the killings. Instead, he argued he was suffering from depression, which led to his actions. Among the aggravating factors, according to his attorneys, was White's high consumption of sugar—in what came to be called the "Twinkie defense." While the jury did not buy that justification in full, it did return a verdict that was considerably less than first-degree murder. They found White guilty of two counts of voluntary manslaughter.[20] For the city's gay community especially, this was an affront.

The response was immediate. A crowd of upward of five thousand, mostly gay men and women, marched to city hall. They were not peaceful. People cheered as demonstrators beat on the building's glass door panels with long metal rods. At the same time, police cars were set afire and firebombs were thrown through the now broken windows of city hall. For their part, police had to use overturned tables to protect themselves from rocks and other objects that were thrown at them.[21] The crowd was having none of it; in near lynch-mob mode, they chanted, "We want White!" It was fury, though one grounded in politics. As one slogan put it, "Dan White, Hit Man for the New Right."[22]

The police, who had been caught off guard at city hall, retaliated. Later that evening they descended on the Castro District, the heart of San Francisco's gay community. As author Mike Weiss recounts, "The baby blues descended on Castro Street with four cops in every car. Word of what was happening brought gays spilling out of the crowded bars onto the sidewalk. 'Go Home!' they chanted. 'Go Home!' and 'Our Street!' A blue line began to swoop down the broad thoroughfare, ducking bottles lobbed from the rooftops."[23] What followed was an ugly counterattack: "A cop went berserk and charged in the chanting homosexuals on the sidewalk. Another screamed, 'Motherfucking faggots,' as he thrashed and spun laying waste. 'Sick cocksuckers,' he was wailing. Other policemen ran to back him up. When the cops retreated, men lay on the sidewalk beaten and bloody." One Police captain remarked, "We lost the battle of City Hall, but we're not going to lose this one."[24]

Outside San Francisco City Hall, May 21, 1979. Photo: Daniel Nicoletta.

Retaliation or not, the two-sided nature of the tumultuous scene underscored that things were not going back to the status quo.

The action in San Francisco was followed by an energized movement on the part of gay and lesbian people, albeit one within more acceptable political bounds. In New York that June—on the tenth anniversary of the 1969 Stonewall Riots in New York—upward of a hundred thousand people marched to commemorate the event. At the same time, a reported two hundred thousand marched in San Francisco. This was followed by a national protest, with more modest numbers (anywhere from 75,000 to 100,000) in Washington, DC.[25] For his part, Jerry Falwell responded by saying that homosexuality was "an outright assault on the family." Battle lines for an intransigent culture war were being laid down. They would not disappear anytime soon.

# 11

# A Shifting Chessboard

I encouraged the Chinese to
support Pol Pot.

—NATIONAL SECURITY ADVISER
ZBIGNIEW BRZEZINSKI, 1979

The Vietnam War may have ended for the United States, but the contention that gave rise to it—the conflict between the United States and the Soviet Union—had not. More precisely, the very fact of defeat for the United States in Vietnam laid the ground for a spiraling escalation of conflict between the two superpowers. This would see numerous milestones between 1978 and 1979.

In East Asia, China had gone from being a chief adversary of the United States to its ally. At the same time, the struggle in Southeast Asia would see previously unimaginable developments. And in the Western Hemisphere, long a safe domain of U.S. domination, things were upended, first in tiny Grenada, then Nicaragua, and then El Salvador. All of this would shatter the complacency that had set in during the relative languor of the mid-seventies.

## Vietnam Invades Cambodia

On Christmas Day 1978, Vietnam sent 150,000 troops into Democratic Kampuchea (formerly Cambodia). Within two weeks, they had driven out Pol Pot's Khmer Rouge government, further tilting the balance of power in Southeast Asia. The action, nominally about border clashes between Vietnamese and Khmer troops and the latter's attacks on Vietnamese civilians, was one act in a multistage power play in a part of the world that saw former allies squaring off in bloody battle.[1]

Throughout the Vietnam War, the Vietnamese had taken aid from both China and the Soviet Union. It was a highly fraught situation given China and the Soviets had been involved in escalating hostilities throughout the decade. This began with acrimonious polemics and culminated in a border dispute in 1969 that brought the two nuclear powers to the precipice of war.[2] At issue between the two self-proclaimed socialist countries was that China saw the Soviets as revisionist and the Soviets saw the Chinese as challenging their socialist authority. Underneath this was a mix of sharp differences in ideology, economic doctrine, and no small amount of national chauvinism.

All of this contributed to the conditions for China's rapprochement with the United States, which began with Nixon's visit to the country in the winter of 1972. That visit presaged a fundamental shift in the state of the Cold War. No longer was the United States contending with a unified socialist bloc of China and the Soviet Union. It now needed only to be concerned with the latter. For its part, China was no longer operating alone in its contention with the Soviet Union.

Throughout the seventies, the Chinese had been adopting a foreign policy in keeping with their view that the Soviet Union was their main enemy. As such, the Communist Party leadership had adopted a foreign policy that tended to support anyone opposing the Soviets. Problematically, this put them in league with dictators such as Ferdinand Marcos in the Philippines and the Shah of Iran. This was on display in September 1978—at a moment when Iran was about to enter a popular revolution—when Chinese premier Hua Guofeng traveled to Tehran. While there he showered praises on the hated Shah: "Today, under the leadership of His Imperial Majesty the Shahan shah, the Iranian people have scored gratifying successes in safeguarding the country's independence and sovereignty, protecting their national resources, and building their country. Iran is playing a role of increasing importance in international affairs."[3] For those around the world who looked to China as something of a beacon for national liberation, it was a bitter pill.

For its part, Vietnam, an uneasy ally of China during its war with the United States, had become wholly aligned with the Soviet Union. The resulting tension between the two countries was on sharp display in polemics published in *Peking Review* at the time of the Kampuchea invasion. In a January 1979 editorial titled "Hanoi's Bellicose Bleating," the Chinese quoted Vietnam's military leader Vo Nguyen Giap, who said his country aimed to "defeat the reactionary clique in Phnom Penh."[4] He then went on to attack China: "The reactionaries in the Peking authorities are practicing big-nation expansionism and hegemonism and colluding with imperialism and the worse reactionaries."[5] There was to be no room for moderation or compromise.

Cambodia had long been an ally of China—a situation that continued under the leadership of the Khmer Rouge, despite that regime's murderous proclivities. As a result, they took the Vietnamese invasion as being against their interests. As the January editorial framed it, "This Moscow-Hanoi duet shows that a deal has been struck between master and flunkey. This is a grave factor in the present situation in Southeast Asia. It proves that people are not overcautious when they consider the Soviet-Vietnam treaty as a military alliance."[6] In their view, the Vietnamese were "regional hegemonists" serving the "global hegemonists behind them, the men in the Kremlin."[7]

For its part, the United States, which had been driven out of Vietnam in 1975, retained geopolitical aims in the region. While they opposed the Soviets and the Vietnamese control of Kampuchea/Cambodia, openly embracing Pol Pot's brutal regime was problematic. As a result, they supported a United Nations resolution denouncing Vietnam while making public denunciations of the Khmer Rouge. As former national security adviser Zbigniew Brzezinski put it, "I encouraged the Chinese to support Pol Pot. Pol Pot was an abomination. We could never support him, but China could."[8] It was a stunning statement, underscoring the ruthless nature of the contention.

## China Invades Vietnam

On January 29, Deng Xiaoping began his historic visit to the United States where, among other things, he had high-level meetings with Jimmy Carter, attended a rodeo in Texas, and met with the wife of slain civil rights leader Martin Luther King.[9] It made for good photo ops but belied darker things on Deng's mind as he toured the country. This became clear when he returned to Beijing in February and turned his attention to teaching Vietnam "a lesson."[10] The lesson he had in mind was an invasion carried out by a force of a half million troops.[11]

The official reason China gave for its actions was that Vietnam had conducted armed incursions that threatened the security of China's southern border. However, as an article in *Peking Review* made clear, Vietnam's actions in Kampuchea were a critical part of the calculus for the Chinese actions: "While launching a massive invasion of Kampuchea and making incessant provocations against China, the Vietnamese authorities have tried to capitalize on its status of a 'small country' for blatant abuses and slanders against China, alleging that China 'harbours ambitions' against Viet Nam, and so on and so forth."[12] As historian Xiaoming Zhang assessed, it was not simply events in Cambodia but Soviet hegemony and the Soviet-Vietnamese alliance that "blended together into a perfect picture of an increasing Soviet threat."[13]

The invasion itself was short lived, lasting only until March, the lesson having been taught. Regardless, the actions of Vietnam and China—putting aside the self-serving rhetoric of anti-hegemonism—were bound up with national and great power contention. None of this fit comfortably in the Manichean outlook that had dominated the anti-war movement of the sixties. For those who had staked a good deal on those causes in the previous decade, it was disorienting and dispiriting.

## Grenada

Whereas the United States may have been limited in operating in Southeast Asia, it was not similarly constrained in the Western Hemisphere. As such, it was not going to tolerate Soviet interference in "its backyard," a resolution that was soon tested.

The challenge came in March of 1979 on the island nation of Grenada. Grenada had been until 1974 a colony of Britain, though it had gained full autonomy in 1967. Colony or not, at a size of 134 square miles and with a population of just over eighty-eight thousand, it did not register as a major site of geopolitical contention. However, a coup in March 1979 changed that. The coup, against the authoritarian leader Sir Charles Gairy by a group of leftists known as the New Jewel Movement, thrust it into the spotlight.

The leader of the movement and the new government was Maurice Bishop. The *New York Times*, though noting that "coups d'état are unusual in the English-speaking Caribbean," was nonetheless conditionally supportive of the new regime, though it cautioned the need for "political reconciliation and economic reconstruction." However, the reconstruction that took shape in the following few years involved support from Cuba, a country whose government the United States loathed. As a result, Grenada would soon fall within the crosshairs of the United States, this at a moment when it was keen to dispel the Vietnam syndrome, to say nothing of its particular intolerance for Marxism in the Western Hemisphere. While culminating events in Grenada were down the road by a few years, the trajectory toward direct United States intervention had been set in motion.[14]

# Nicaragua

While Grenada was one kind of unwelcome situation, another soon emerged on the other side of the Caribbean Sea. In 1979, the Somoza family had ruled over Nicaragua for forty-five years. That ended in July that year when Anastasio Somoza Debayle was forced to leave the country. For the Somoza family, it was the end of their legacy. For the United States, it meant the loss of a safe and reliable U.S. regime.

Since the mid-seventies, Somoza and his National Guard had been engaged in an ongoing civil war with the socialist Frente Sandinista de Liberación Nacional (FSLN). In January 1978, the conflict hit a major turning point with the killing of Pedro Joaquin Chamorro, publisher of Nicaragua's only independent newspaper, *La Prensa*. That killing led to—among other things—a general strike on January 28, 1978, which is reported to have closed down 80–85 percent of the country.[15]

That tumult energized the FSLN guerillas fighting the regime, who launched an offensive aimed at overthrowing Somoza. At the end of May, they projected it would be three months before they could take the capital, however matters sped up considerably. On July 17, Somoza fled the country. He traveled first to Miami, but he confronted the prospect of being denied asylum. As a result, he left the United States a month later to take up residence in Paraguay. His exile would be short lived—he was assassinated the following year.[16] The tumult his exit initiated, however, was only beginning. It would spill deep into the next decade.

## El Salvador

The political earthquake in Nicaragua sent ripples into nearby El Salvador. The most densely populated country in Central America, El Salvador's four million people lived on just over eight thousand square miles of land. General Carlos Humberto Romero, who had been controversially elected president in 1977, served the interests of a small land-owning oligarchy, the so-called 14 Families, who controlled the majority of land and wealth in the country.

Tensions, however, were running high in 1979, to the point that on October 15 a section of young military officers—with the backing of the United States—overthrew Romero's government. While the new government ostensibly claimed it would stand for reform, the reality was otherwise. Within two weeks of seizing power, forces of the new regime opened fire on a demonstration organized by a coalition known as the Frente de Acción Popular Unificada. Two people were killed.[17] The outrage at the killings threw fuel on an insurgency already underway, leading the forces waging a guerilla war to redouble their efforts. That, along with events in Nicaragua, fed the belief that change was in the wind. As the slogan proclaimed, "If Nicaragua was victorious, so too will be El Salvador."[18]

Events in the Caribbean and Central America were still developing in 1979. They were nonetheless harbingers of a protracted period of instability, insurgency, and civil war.

## Fires Everywhere

The above were all hotspots that would profoundly impact the end period of the Cold War, but they were not the only places where stark contention was playing out. In October, the South Korean president, Park Chung Hee, and his chief bodyguard and aide were assassinated by the head of the Korean Central Intelligence Agency (KCIA), Kim Jae Kyu. The killing came amid demonstrations against Park's repressive regime. The shooting took place inside the KCIA dining room after an argument between the two men, where Park criticized the KCIA's role in suppressing demonstrations.[19]

Further west, in Northern Ireland, the battle between Irish nationalists and Britain would continue with unabated intensity. In March, Airey Neave, a Conservative member of Parliament, was killed when a bomb planted in his car by the Irish National Liberation Army exploded as he was leaving Parliament.[20] That was followed by the IRA's August assassination of Lord Mountbatten and members of his family (see Chapter 7). These targeted killings were added to a list that included bombings and attacks on British soldiers throughout Northern Ireland.

In Southern Africa, the African National Congress and other anti-apartheid forces would continue to wage struggle—both armed and in the realm of public opinion—against the racist apartheid system. The *New York Times* reported that in the spring of 1979 "guerilla incidents are on the rise in the northern Transvaal." The disruption hit every sphere of the country, including forcing rural whites to relocate to cities, leaving at least 25 percent of border-area farms unoccupied. At the same time, the war was spreading to the cities, including a bombing at an affluent shopping area in downtown Johannesburg that injured several whites. As the *New York Times* noted, "Such bombings, as well as fatal shootings and arson, are increasing."[21]

Meantime, in what had been the white-ruled African country of Rhodesia, major change was underway. As a result of the success of the liberation forces of the Black majority, the country entered a transitional phase, first becoming Zimbabwe-Rhodesia, a situation that would last till year's end, before transforming into fully Black-rule Zimbabwe in 1980.[22] All of this was headed for its denouement, in Zimbabwe sooner than in South Africa, but white rule in that part of Africa was in its final phase.

On the surface, these invasions, border attacks, and civil wars would appear to occupy their own universes, containing the multitude of contradictions that exist within nations and intranational conflicts. However, in 1979 all of this was also freighted with the much bigger contention between the United States and the Soviet Union. As events raced toward the year's end, matters would reach a tipping point.

# 12

# The Looming
# 1980s

The erosion of our confidence
in the future is threatening to
destroy the social and political
fabric of America.

—**PRESIDENT JIMMY CARTER**,
July 15, 1979

On December 8, 1979, the Soviet Union dispatched a brigade of air-borne troops—about two thousand soldiers—to Bagram Airbase outside Kabul, Afghanistan. It was the first in a wave of deployments that by the end of the month saw two divisions, around twenty-six thousand troops, in the country. By February 1980 it was estimated the Soviets had seven divisions in Afghanistan.[1] The short-term impetus for the deployment was stabilizing a Soviet client state that teetered on the cusp of being lost. On a larger plane, however, it was but one move among a multitude in which the contention between the United States and the Soviet Union was reaching a fever pitch. At stake was not simply the overall global order but, in the direst scenarios, the future of humanity.

The spark for the Soviet invasion was a power struggle in Afghanistan within the leadership of the ruling party, the pro-Soviet People's Democratic Party of Afghanistan (PDPA). Specifically, the contention was between Hafizullah Amin, the country's prime minister, and Noor Mohammad Taraki, the general secretary of the PDPA.[2] The former had increasingly alienated both the Afghan population and his Soviet benefactors. The Soviets were worried he would lose all legitimacy due to his use of harsh and murderous repression against his enemies. In turn, they feared they would lose their foothold in this strategically located country nestled between Soviet Central Asia and Iran. To their way of thinking, Taraki was better suited to lead. Unfortunately for them, Amin disagreed.

What transpired was an unsuccessful assassination attempt on Amin by his political opponents in September 1979. In response Amin, later that month, initiated a full-on coup in which Taraki was arrested. He was executed three weeks later. That was the final straw for the Soviets. For them, Amin—who was flirting with both the United States and Muslim rebels—could have conceivably switched allegiances. As such, he needed to be removed forcefully.[3]

The result was the airlifting of a massive number of troops into Bagram, followed by a Soviet coup. This was accomplished by the dispatch of a full division of Soviet troops to Kabul's Darulaman Palace. There they proceeded to kill the guards, destroy the tanks, and finally kill Amin—the KGB had earlier that month failed twice in trying to poison him.[4] With Amin gone, the Soviets installed Babrak Karmal, a former leader of the PDPA who had been driven by Amin into exile in Prague.[5] Two days later, two more divisions of Soviet troops crossed the border into Afghanistan, one headed for Kabul, the other for the southern city of Kandahar. The Soviet occupation of Afghanistan had begun. It would go on for a decade and would ultimately be a critical factor in the collapse of the Soviet empire in 1989.

## A Soviet Vietnam

The United States had been following events in Afghanistan closely. It understood the difficulties the Soviets confronted and proactively moved to exacerbate them. As such, it had begun supporting the Muslim opposition to the pro-Soviet regime—even before the invasion. In a 1998 interview with the French paper *Le Nouvel Observateur*, Carter's national security adviser Zbigniew Brzezinski laid this out:

> According to the official version of history, CIA aid to the Mujahedin began during 1980, that is to say, after the Soviet army invaded Afghanistan on December 24, 1979. But the reality, closely guarded until now, is completely otherwise. Indeed, it was July 3, 1979, that President Carter signed the first directive for secret aid to the opponents of the pro-Soviet regime in Kabul. And that very day, I wrote a note to the president in which I explained to him that in my opinion, this aid was going to induce a Soviet military intervention.[6]

Brzezinski, cl'early proud of the effort, added, "That secret operation was an excellent idea. It had the effect of drawing the Russians into the Afghan trap. . . . We now [had] the opportunity of giving to the USSR its Vietnam war."[7] A similar note was struck by the *New York Times*. In the wake of Taraki's assassination, the paper reported, "Some months ago, an American returning from Afghanistan gleefully described the already decaying situation there as "the Russian Vietnam."[8]

The Vietnam scenario, where the Soviets found themselves at war with an entire population aided by a major power, did play out. Oleg Vershinin, a former Soviet "black beret" special services officer who served in Afghanistan in the 1980s, described how things

Soviet Soldiers in Kabul, Afghanistan. Photo: U.S. Department of Defense (U.S. Government).

looked on the ground: "More than once we advanced on some kishlyak (village) only to find it completely empty. We'd do a thorough search of all the houses and find nothing. Then we'd come out and see the pickets we'd posted lying face down in the dust, dead. Other times, we'd move to break camp in the morning, and one of our guys would be wrapped in his blanket with his throat cut."[9] Another soldier, Sergei Bondar, a captain in a motorized infantry division stationed in Herat and Kandahar in the mid-1980s, put it starkly: "The only thing the Afghans hate more than each other is a foreigner. They will unite against any outsider, and the result will be a long, bloody story with no happy ending."[10] Pointedly, Bondar's assessment was lost on the then benefactors of the Mujahadeen. The United States would one day find itself in the same position.

That, however, was for the future. Much like the loss of its ally the Shah, the Soviet invasion of Afghanistan presented the United States with a critical geopolitical challenge. While it may have seen an opportunity with the Soviets bogged down in a Vietnam-type conflict—as imprecise as that analogy may have been—there was also considerable danger. As Jimmy Carter made clear in a statement soon after the invasion, "A Soviet-occupied Afghanistan threatens both Iran and Pakistan and is a steppingstone to possible control over much of the world's oil supplies."[11] These were, put plainly, the highest of stakes.

At work was a dynamic that heightened the tensions in a Cold War that were quickly shunting to the side notions of détente and replacing them with confrontation. As historian Barnett Rubin observed, "The Soviets thought that if the [Afghan] state were to dissolve in this way, it would create a power vacuum that the United States would try to fill, since they [the United States] had just lost their most important ally in the region, the Shah of Iran. With typical paranoia, the Soviets overestimated what the US was doing, just as the US, also in a paranoid way, thought that the Soviets planned to seize Afghanistan and then march on to the Persian Gulf. Neither of these perceptions was true, of course."[12] Such misconceptions aside, Afghanistan decisively shattered détente and the relative calm that had been in place. The Soviet invasion of Afghanistan transformed the Cold War into a shooting war, albeit by proxy, between the United States and the Soviet Union.

## Carter for President

Events in Afghanistan came amid the launching of the 1980 presidential campaign in the United States. Jimmy Carter had become president on the heels of the Watergate scandal. His ascension represented an effort by the ruling authorities—as rivalrous as they were among themselves—to repair the damage not only of Watergate but the fallout of the Vietnam War.

Carter's hallmark was a campaign for "human rights." The impetus, as he described it in his 1977 inaugural, was that "because we are free, we can never be indifferent to the fate of freedom elsewhere." On the surface, it seemed a benign, even worthy undertaking. However, as one columnist put it, "The ratio of good intentions, compared to accomplishments, is unusually high."[13]

More than anything, the campaign was about restoring the legitimacy of the United States in a world in which its reputation had taken a serious hit after the bloody conflict in Vietnam and the exposure of its coups and dirty schemes from Cuba to Indonesia to Chile to Iran.[14] However, Carter was not operating in a world in which the Cold War contradictions that had led them to undertake such measures had disappeared. True, the United States no longer had to deal with the dual antagonism of China *and* the Soviet Union, but dealing with *only* the Soviet empire was going to be formidable. And it had to do this simultaneously while dealing with its own economic problems. Along with this were the newly emerging crises in Iran, Central America, Afghanistan, and elsewhere. If one believed in curses, Carter would have been a good subject of such an affliction.

In that respect, it is worth pointing out that something otherwise was happening than is generally assumed. The dominant view of the seventies is that it was a time of the "rise of conservatism," as if it were something of an innate impulse on the part of the "American people"—the wants and needs of the "American people" being the standard invocation by politicians when pursuing a particular agenda. Less acknowledged is the underlying material basis for all this—the ruling elites, spread over both political parties, attempting to navigate the pre-eminent challenge to their empire, the United States' contention with the Soviet Union, and the need to take the gloves off in order to do this.

Jimmy Carter, who came into office proclaiming a more moral America and as a champion of human rights, found himself by the end of 1979 transformed. It was he who initiated funding of Islamist guerillas in Afghanistan, developed new nuclear weapons, welcomed the despised Shah of Iran into the country, and tacitly supported the Pol Pot regime against Vietnam.

Despite all this, by decade's end the powers, broadly defined, confronted a situation that compelled them to ascend to another level. This was the context in which Ronald Reagan stepped onto the geopolitical stage.

# Reagan

Ronald Reagan earned his political stripes as the hardline governor of California, intent on quashing civil disorders, especially on the campuses. His attitude came out tellingly in a letter to a friend in 1966: "How far do we go in tolerating these people and this trash under the excuse of academic freedom and freedom of expression? . . . We wouldn't let a LeRoi Jones [Amiri Baraka] in our living room and we wouldn't tolerate this kind of language in front of our families."[15] It was rhetoric backed up by action, as when he sent in 2,200 National Guard troops onto the University of California, Berkeley, campus during the contention around People's Park in 1969.[16]

Reagan, among other things, was the embodiment of the anti-sixties movement, intent on steering the country back to the type of ethos that existed in the Eisenhower years. As part of his 1980 campaign for president, he gave a speech in Philadelphia, Mississippi, where a Black man, James Chaney, and his two white comrades Andrew Goodman and Michael Schwerner were murdered in 1964 by racists while organizing for civil rights. In his speech, Regan declared, "I believe in states' rights," a well-understood code for white supremacy in the southern states.[17] Beyond that, his program was effectively neoliberal, advocating the shrinking of the federal government, reducing taxes—especially on the rich—and eliminating governmental regulations. All of which benefited the wealthiest individuals and corporations in the country.

Of a more immediate consequence, however, was Reagan's view on the United States' place in the world. In this he offered an argument against those—he did not say who—who say, "The United States, like other great civilizations of the past, has reached the zenith of its power." Following that, he made clear that the United States was on a course to advance—by knocking down its main adversary for global empire: "During a time when the Soviet Union may enjoy nuclear superiority over this country, we must never waiver in our commitment to our allies nor accept any negotiation which is not clearly in the national interest. We must judge carefully. Though we should leave no initiative untried in our pursuit of peace, we must be clear voiced in our resolve to resist any unpeaceful act wherever it may occur."[18] The notion that the Soviets had nuclear superiority was a trope invoked since John F. Kennedy ran for president, in what was then erroneously argued as "a missile gap."[19] That aside, Reagan's speech was a provocation. While the United States might be open to détente-like negotiations, the threat was the real statement. The United States would "resist any unpeaceful act wherever it may occur." Reagan had laid down the markers that would come to inform his presidency.

## Talkin' World War III

In certain ways, a third world war had been going on since 1949. From the Greek Civil War, the Korean War, and the Vietnam War to proxy conflicts and crises in the Congo, Indonesia, Ethiopia, Angola, and the Dominican Republic to the Berlin Crisis, the Cuban Missile Crisis, and beyond. Still, the actual squaring off of U.S. troops against those of the Soviet Union, to say nothing of a nuclear exchange, had thus far been avoided.

As the seventies wore on, however, the U.S. government was systematically preparing for nuclear war—from constructing new weapons to establishing agencies such as FEMA in order to withstand the full effects of a possible attack. Along with this, elements were entering the cultural realm that had the effect of preparing people for the awful possibility of such a war.

In 1978, General Sir John Hackett (ret.), with the help of a number of his colleagues, published a fact-based fictional account of World War III. The book, *The Third World War: August 1985*, rode the bestsellers list for a good portion of 1979.[20] What was compelling—and disturbing—about Hackett's book, beyond the fact of its mere existence, was its scenario of a world war far short of Armageddon. His story was not one of scattered survivors emerging from their bunker confronting rubble. Neither was it the dystopian landscape of fierce survivors contending à la *Mad Max*, the small-budget Australian box office smash that year. Rather, Hackett envisioned a war that could be *won*.

Specifically, in Hackett's telling, only the English city of Birmingham and the Soviet city of Minsk were destroyed—Moscow and Washington, DC, were unscathed. The book was essentially a valentine to the importance of NATO—unsurprising given Hackett had been a NATO commander in the sixties. In that respect, he was quite upfront. When asked about it "being propaganda for NATO," he responded, "I agree. But I don't see anything wrong with that. My whole purpose is to tell a cautionary tale and that if we don't do better, there is an ogre just around the corner. That ogre is war by inadvertence."[21] Such good intentions considered, his book still acted as a psychological tool preparing people for the awesome possibility of World War III.

Another book, this one wholly a work of fiction, told a different story. In a preview teasing Fredrick Forsyth's forthcoming novel *The Devil's Alternative* (1979) the *New York Times* reported, "Among the ingredients the author has thrown into the hopper are a failed Russian grain crop, a group of Ukrainian terrorists at the end of their tether, a strategic arms agreement teetering into failure, a supertanker that has been hijacked and is waiting to pollute the North Sea, a Politburo full of internal feuds; [and] a looming World War III."[22] Such sensationalism is the stuff of popular fiction. However, the buttons pushed were revealing of what was under consideration by those fiction writers whose work necessitated understanding the cutting edge of military preparations and secretive governmental operations.

Such thoughts on World War III were not confined to quasi-fiction or fiction. Journalists also got in the act. The *Christian Science Monitor* in a piece about the current situation—from Iran to Vietnam's invasion of Cambodia—noted, "The distance between the Soviet border and Tehran is about the same as that between Washington and New York. Consequently, if the

Soviets tried to pull anything here, the danger of direct Soviet involvement would be all the greater." It then suggested that such a move could spark U.S. intervention, "which presumably Moscow does not want unless it is prepared to spark World War III."[23] A similar theme was struck the following month when the paper opined on China's invasion of Vietnam: "Behind all these calculations is China's deep concern that consolidation of a united Vietnamese-dominated Indochina backed by the Soviet Union, would hasten the day of World War III."[24]

In some respects, this was fanciful, and taken in isolation could be dismissed as writers and journalists attempting to capture people's attention. On a more fundamental level, however, it reflected what had been set loose in the ether after the tumultuous events of the previous year.

In early December 1979, *Chicago Tribune* columnist Robert Cross wrote a piece in which he struggled to make sense of the decade coming to an end. He wrote, "Either this was a decade that could not be squeezed into a tiny epoch, or we're going through a vast epoch that cannot be confined to a decade."[25] His was a provocative construction that captured something essential about that complex and mercurial period. Looking back, the seventies were less sui generis than a stepping stone on the road to a greater resolution. As such, by 1979 a threshold had been crossed, the decade that had existed was fading into the mists of the past. The final conflicts of the Cold War lay ahead.

# Conclusion

On New Year's Day in 1980, anyone expecting a message of love and fellowship from Pope John Paul II was in for a disappointment. In his New Year's homily, the pontiff pointed out that "only 200 of the 50,000 nuclear bombs that are estimated to exist already would be enough to destroy the major part of the largest cities of the world." The pope did not, however, suggest any action to prevent such Armageddon beyond "prayers for peace"—a practice of dubious efficacy.[1]

The same day the pope delivered his remarks, thousands of Afghanis and their supporters living in Iran stormed the Soviet embassy in Tehran. The mood was such that protestors tore "the Soviet flag into pieces with their teeth and hands" before setting the shreds on fire.

Meantime, on Iran's eastern border, the United States was giving millions of dollars and shipping matériel in support of the radical Muslims of the Mujahadeen in Afghanistan to fight against the Soviets. The CIA even cooked up a scheme to translate the Qu'ran into Uzbek and ship copies into Soviet-occupied territory to help fuel the Muslim insurgency.[2]

Back in the United States, Ronald Reagan was on course to be elected president. Reagan would pitch his presidency as "Morning in America," a euphemism for a country that would take a far more aggressive stance on the global stage, from funding anti-communist guerillas in Nicaragua and supporting death squads in El Salvador to overthrowing the popular government of Maurice Bishop in

Grenada. Along with this, billions of dollars would be appropriated to the Pentagon to escalate an arms race that would either wreck the Soviet Union financially or, failing that, potentially annihilate it with advanced weaponry. The calendar may have turned the page by a single day on January 1, but the United States and the world had entered a new era.

As has been shown here, the seventies of popular understanding ended well before the calendar decade in which it resided. From roughly November 1978 on, events began to assume a different character from the period immediately preceding them.

While the horror in Jonestown and the murders of George Moscone and Harvey Milk in San Francisco City Hall may have registered at the time mainly for their shock value, they nonetheless concentrated contradictions that were sharpening as the seventies drew to a close. And they came amid a shifting geopolitical framework—the unprecedented upheaval in Iran, instability in Afghanistan, and tectonic changes in China.

As for Jimmy Carter, who had become president as a conciliator out to repair the damage of the Vietnam War and Watergate, the unprecedented challenge of the 1973 Oil Crisis, and the delegitimating actions of the Nixon administration, he found himself consumed in his last years in office by the U.S. contention with the Soviet Union. As such, a president aiming to stand on a platform of human rights was transformed into a Cold Warrior of the first order. In this, he would implement measures and policies as chilling, if not more so, than any that had come before. Carter is often cast as a certain embodiment of the self-absorbed seventies, when in fact events necessitated an almost Jekyll and Hyde transformation.

While disco, polyester suits, and lava lamps may still have proliferated, the culture of numbification was being challenged, and generally not in a good way. From the poison politics of the Moral Majority to the popularization of aggressive nationalism and xenophobia in the wake of hostage-taking in Iran, the "Me Decade" was being replaced by an aggressively reactionary social and political environment.

All of this took place amid the slipping away of the United States' industrial base, which was tearing up a way of life millions had come to take for granted. Arguably, and more consequentially, it was chipping away at the very basis of America's claim to global domination: its unparalleled ability to manufacture and the wealth that derived from that. And that change was a result of a good many other countries stepping into the breach. Chief among them would be China, which was renouncing the Maoist precepts of communism toward "socialism with Chinese characteristics." As such, it was laying the groundwork to become the world's biggest manufacturer, making it a far more powerful country than it had been throughout the twentieth century.[3]

While many of the elements from that time have passed into oblivion—most pointedly the Soviet Union is no more—their lasting impact is enduring. We find ourselves today with a diminished and riven United States, one whose future power—while by no means predetermined—is in question. Simultaneously, the internal changes that brought China into an alliance with the United States have created a situation where it has become the latter's peer economically and, increasingly, geopolitically, holding the prospect of challenging the United States' hegemonic role. Where all this— and the multitude of other contradictions percolating—leads, is beyond anyone's ability to say.

What can be said is the changes that manifested themselves in the final months of the seventies—a decade often ridiculed for its lack of seriousness—have been enduring. As such, they demand our fullest comprehension as we navigate the challenges, perils, and unpredictability that lie ahead.

# Coda

---

## The Soviet Union and China

The Soviet Union exited Afghanistan in February 1989 after a decade of bloody conflict. Two years later the Soviet Union collapsed, leaving the United States, for the moment, as the world's most powerful unchallenged empire. While the Communist Party was losing power in the Soviet Union, in China a major challenge to Deng Xiaoping's rule occurred with a mass demonstration between April and June 1989 in Tiananmen Square. The protest would be put down violently, with hundreds, perhaps thousands, killed—there has been no official death toll.[1] In its wake, China proceeded even more aggressively down the capitalist road and is today the world's second-largest economy—after the United States.

## Iran

The U.S. hostages held in Iran were released on January 20, 1980. There continues to be debate over whether or not president-to-be Ronald Reagan brokered a deal to delay their release in order to hinder the chances of Jimmy Carter winning a second term. True or not, the debate mistakenly focuses on the hostage crisis—rather than the loss of Iran as a reliable ally, as the more consequential issue in Carter's defeat.[2] Regardless, with the resolution of that crisis, Ayatollah Khomeini and the Islamists grouped around him consolidated power in Iran and set about jailing and killing the secular opposition to their rule.[3] Soon after consolidating power, the country entered into one of the bloodiest conflicts of the1980s, a war against Iraq. It was a war that saw the United States, at different points, aid both sides. The conflict lasted until 1988, with the loss of a half million lives and over a million casualties.[4]

## Nuclear Power and Anthrax

In 1986, there was a nuclear accident at the Chernobyl power plant in the Soviet Republic of Ukraine in which a reactor exploded. Within hours of the blast, two people had died from radiation poisoning and at least twenty-eight others died over the course of the next several months. The area remains a dead zone sealed off from human habitation.

Twenty-five years later, in the immediate wake of the attack on the World Trade Center in 2001, the United States confronted a weaponized anthrax attack that killed five and sickened seventeen others. The attack, while still shrouded in mystery, is thought to have been undertaken by an estranged U.S. scientist who sent the deadly pathogen through the mail.[5]

## The Economy

Since its 1979 peak, manufacturing employment in the United States has considerably declined. In June 2019, the number of people working in industry was 12.8 million, a decrease of 6.7 million—or 35 percent—from its highest point. The trend continues. In contrast, China in 2022 was the world's largest manufacturer, accounting for 20 percent of all global output—the United States is now in second place at 18 percent.[6]

## The Radicals

In the aftermath of the demonstration against Deng Xiaoping, while still facing charges (later to be dropped) the RCP's Bob Avakian fled the country where he unsuccessfully sought political asylum in France.[7] He nonetheless continued his self-exile during the ensuing decades. Avakian re-emerged on the U.S. scene in the mid-2000s to lead what remained of the RCP.

After the killing of the CWP members in Greensboro, there were two criminal trials, one state, and one federal. Both ended in the acquittal of the white supremacists charged. A wrongful death suit, brought by the surviving victims, resulted in an award of $350,000.[8] The group itself dissolved in 1985, transforming into the New Democratic Movement, which itself dissolved a few years later.[9]

As for MOVE, with the destruction of their Powelton Village home in 1978, the remaining members of the group resettled in a house in West Philadelphia. On May 13, 1985, however, there was an even bloodier incident. Police, responding to neighbors' complaints about the agitation by MOVE via loudspeakers, laid siege to the house. Matters culminated in the dropping of a bomb on an ad hoc bunker built atop the residence. This in turn set off a fire that would consume the MOVE house, killing eleven men, women, and children inside. The out-of-control fire also destroyed the homes of the entire block on which the house stood.[10] The incident led to recriminations and investigations. The city would be forced to pay $1.5 million to Ramona Africa, who survived the attack, and the relatives of two others killed, along with a $12.83 million settlement to the residents who lost their homes as a result of the government dropping a bomb in a residential neighborhood.[11]

## Terrorism

In 1981, remnants of the BLA and WU robbed a Brink's truck of $1.6 million in Nyack, New York, killing one of the guards in the process. What followed was the systematic, if protracted, rolling up of the remnants of the former underground revolutionaries, including Kathy Boudin, Judith Clark, Sekou Odinga, Marilyn Buck, David Gilbert, and Mutulu Shakur—all of whom would serve decades in prison.[12] Assata Shakur remains free, living in exile in Cuba.

## The Moral Majority

The Moral Majority expanded its reach throughout the 1980s and was part of the coalition that brought Ronald Reagan to power. The evangelical movement of which it was a part would continue to play an important role in Republican politics, including supporting the ascent of Donald Trump and the ever-sharpening divisions within U.S. politics.

## Nicaragua, El Salvador, and Grenada

The fraught situation in Central America saw a bloody civil war in El Salvador that lasted from 1980 to 1992. In Nicaragua, U.S.-funded Contras waged war against the Sandinista government for over a decade. Funding for the Contras would lead to a scandal that neutered the Reagan administration in its final years, this after it became known that they had traded arms to Iran for money to sustain its mercenary army.

In the Caribbean, in 1983 the United States launched an invasion of Grenada to topple the government of Maurice Bishop, heralding, in its view, "the end of the Vietnam Syndrome." This was a proclamation it would reprise again, through an invasion of

Panama in 1990, and two wars in Iraq—the first in 1990–1991, the second between 2003 and 2011. Also, in the wake of the terrorist bombing of the World Trae Center in September 2001, the United States overthrew the government of the Taliban in Afghanistan, leading to a twenty-year occupation of that country. That occupation ended in a U.S. withdrawal in 2021, at which point the Taliban again assumed control.[13]

# Acknowledgments

A word of thanks to those who helped this work get realized. To Conor Gallagher for his long-standing support and for helping me work through key ideas. To Trevor Griffey for his thoughts and insights on the shifting economic topography. To Terry Leonard and Laurie Malkoff for taking the time to read the manuscript, pointing out errors, and offering their impressions and insights. To John Wezalis for his help in researching the fate of Standard Furniture in the Mohawk Valley. To April Krassner who some years back shepherded me through a research paper on Afghanistan that I was able to draw on for this work. To Nicole Solano and the team at Rutgers University Press for their encouragement and support in this project. And to Irka Mateo, my life partner and editor-in-chief, who helped me work through two hundred iterations of the title and everything after. That said, the work and analysis here are wholly mine.

# Notes

## Preface

1 Neil Genzliner, "Delbert Africa, 74, Convicted in Radical Group's Clash with Police, Dies," *New York Times*, June 17, 2020; Associated Press, "Last Member of MOVE Freed on Parole in Death of Officer," *WHYY*, February 7, 2020, https://whyy.org/articles/last-member-of -move-freed-on-parole-in-death-of-officer/.

## Introduction

1 Martin Weill, "A Little Revelry, Some Unconcern Greet New Year," *Washington Post*, January 1, 1978.
2 Jack Anderson, "The Big Stories of 1978," *Washington Post*, January 1, 1978.
3 David S. Broder, "Time for Carter to Come Home," *Washington Post*, January 1, 1978; John Hudson, "David Broder, 'Dean of the Washington Press Corps,' Dies," *Atlantic*, March 9, 2011.
4 Joseph Kraft, "'More of the Same,' for Next Year," *Washington Post*, January 1, 1978.
5 "Oil Embargo, 1973–1974," Office of the Historian, accessed May 19, 2022, https://history.state.gov/milestones/1969-1976/oil-embargo.
6 For background on U.S.-China rapprochement, see "The Opening of China," Richard Nixon Foundation, accessed August 23, 2022, https://www.nixonfoundation.org/exhibit/the-opening-of-china/. See also Norman Kempster, "Nixon Played China Card in Vietnam," *Los Angeles Times*, January 4, 1999.
7 "US Relations with China, 1949–2022," Council on Foreign Relations, accessed August 23, 2022, https://www.cfr.org/timeline/us-relations -china.

8  "U.S. Relations with Egypt," U.S. Department of State, April 29, 2022, https://www.state.gov/u-s-relations-with-egypt/.
9  "The Nobel Peace Prize, 1978," NobelPrize.org, accessed December 27, 2022, https://www.nobelprize.org/prizes/peace/1978/summary/. Karen Elliot House, "Begin and Sadat Sign Historic Agreement," *Wall Street Journal*, September 18, 1978.

## Chapter 1    The Beginning of the End of the 1970s

Epigraph: Jimmy Carter, "The State of the Union Address Delivered before a Joint Session of the Congress," American Presidency Project, January 19, 1978, https://www.presidency.ucsb.edu/documents/the-state-the-union -address-delivered-before-joint-session-the-congress-1.

1  Chris Carlsson, "Peoples Temple: Historical Essay," FoundSF, accessed March 22, 2022, https://www.foundsf.org/index.php?title=Peoples _Temple.
2  John Jacobs, "Jim Jones and His Peoples Temple," *San Francisco Chronicle*, November 19, 1978; Jeff Guinn, *The Road to Jonestown: Jim Jones and His Peoples Temple* (New York: Simon and Schuster, 2017), 336; James Sobredo, "The Battle for the International Hotel," FoundSF, accessed May 3, 2022, https://www.foundsf.org/index.php?title=The _Battle_for_the_International_Hotel; "Demonstration at the International Hotel," *Synapse* [student newspaper of University of California, San Francisco], January 20, 1977.
3  David Chiu, "Jonestown: 13 Things You Should Know about Cult Massacre," *Rolling Stone*, May 29, 2020; Guinn, *Road to Jonestown*, 290–291.
4  "Who Accompanied Congressman Leo Ryan on His Trip to Guyana in November 1978?," Alternative Considerations of Jonestown and Peoples Temple, last modified February 19, 2021, https://jonestown.sdsu.edu/ ?page_id=35350.
5  Guinn, *Road to Jonestown*, 345.
6  Charles Garry and Mark Lane were not on the airstrip during the attack. See Guinn *Road to Jonestown*, 432–436.
7  "Who Was Killed at the Port Kaituma Airstrip on November 18? Who Was Wounded? Who Were Identified as the Assailants?," Alternative Considerations of Jonestown and Peoples Temple, last modified August 27, 2021, https://jonestown.sdsu.edu/?page_id=35346.
8  Guinn, *Roade to Jonestown*, 448.
9  "Rep. Ryan Shot: Ambush at Guyana Airport," *San Francisco Chronicle* [published as *San Francisco Examiner*], November 19, 1978.
10 Fielding M. McGehee III, Jonestown Institute, "Q1053–4 Summary," Alternative Considerations of Jonestown and Peoples Temple, last modified July 10, 2023, https://jonestown.sdsu.edu/?page_id=28022. See also KaiiBaler, "Jim Jones and the Peoples Temple Singing 'The

Internationale,'" YouTube video, July 10, 2021, https://www.youtube
.com/watch?v=BxK9jaHYCK8.

11   Guinn, *Road to Jonestown*, 292–293.

12   Mike Weiss, *Double Play: The San Francisco City Hall Killings* (Boston:
Addison Wesley, 1984), 252–253.

13   Weiss, 252–253.

14   Weiss, 252–253.

15   George Draper, "Moscone, Milk, Slain: Dan White Is Held," *San
Francisco Chronicle*, November 28, 1978.

16   Steve Rubenstein, "A Candlelight Vigil at City Hall," *San Francisco
Chronicle*, November 28, 1978.

17   Linda Charlton, "Clashes and Tear Gas Mar Shah's Welcome in
Capital," *New York Times*, November 16, 1977.

18   "12 Killed in Iran Clashes; Strike Cripples Tehran," *Los Angeles Times*,
November 27, 1978; "25 Iranian Protesters Arrested," *Washington
Post*, November 1, 1978.

19   Hedrick Smith, "US Officials Fearful That Shah May Lose Control,"
*New York Times*, November 6, 1978.

20   Andy Green, "Flashback: The Sex Pistols Come to a Chaotic End,"
*Rolling Stone*, November 20, 2012, https://www.rollingstone.com
/music/music-news/flashback-the-sex-pistols-come-to-a-chaotic-end
-57410/.

21   Janice Headley, "Which Bands Mattered to the 'Only Band That
Matters'?," February 5, 2021, *KEXP*, https://www.kexp.org/read/2021/2
/5/which-bands-mattered-only-band-matters/.

22   While recording in California, Joe Strummer and Mick Jones encountered a painting by Berkeley artist Hugh Brown titled *End of the Trail
for Capitalism*, part of his "Chinese Tourist Art" exhibition. The
painting was inspired by a 1950s postcard featuring a dead cowboy called
"End of the Trail." See "The Clash *Give 'Em Enough Rope* Album Cover
Taken from Old Postcard," *feelnumb* (blog), July 22, 2012, http://web
.archive.org/web/20230206091403/http:/www.feelnumb.com/2012/07
/22/the-clash-give-em-enough-rope-album-cover-taken-from-old
-postcard/; Philip Hoare, "It Wasn't Just the Queen—Pop Music
Borrowed Nazi Symbols Too," *Guardian*, July 23, 2015, https://www
.theguardian.com/commentisfree/2015/jul/23/pop-music-nazi-symbols
-art-queen-fascist.

23   Vivien Goldman, "Never Mind the Swastikas: The Secret of History the
UK's 'Punky Jews,'" *Guardian*, February 27, 2014.

24   Marcus Gray, *The Clash: Return of the Last Gang in Town* (Milwaukee:
Hal Leonard, 2004), 150.

25   Mikal Gilmore, "The Clash: Anger on the Left," *Rolling Stone*,
February 18, 2011, https://www.rollingstone.com/music/music-news/the
-clash-anger-on-the-left-250578/ (originally published 1979).

26 Kevin Klose, "Soviets and Vietnamese Sign Treaty, Warn Chinese," *Washington Post*, November 4, 1978; "Nobel Is Suggested for Sadat and Begin," *New York Times*, November 23, 1977; "U.S. Relations with Egypt," U.S. State Department, accessed December 27, 2022, https://www.state.gov/u-s-relations-with-egypt/; "Soviet A-Test Held," *Los Angeles Times*, November 1, 1978; "U.S.-British A-Test Held," *Los Angeles Times*, November 19, 1978.

## Chapter 2   Marg bar Shah! (Death to the Shah!)

Epigraph: Donald Wilber, *Clandestine Service History: Overthrow of Premier Mossadegh on Iran, November 1952–August 1953*, March 1954, National Security Archive, https://nsarchive2.gwu.edu/NSAEBB/ciacase/Clandestine%20Service%20History.pdf, p. 196. Wilber was a CIA agent and an expert in Persian architecture. He was one of the main planners of the covert operation to overthrow the Iranian prime minister Mohammad Mosaddegh in 1953.

1 Based on the author's 1978 conversation with "Farzad" (not his real name).
2 Lawrence Wu, "How the CIA Overthrew Iran's Democracy in 4 Days," *NPR*, February 7, 2019, https://www.npr.org/2019/01/31/690363402/how-the-cia-overthrew-irans-democracy-in-four-days; "Secret History of the CIA in Iran," *New York Times*, April 16, 2000; "CIA Confirms Role in 1953 Iran Coup," National Security Archive, August 19, 2013, https://nsarchive2.gwu.edu/NSAEBB/NSAEBB435/.
3 "New Findings on Clerical Involvement in the 1953 Coup in Iran," National Security Archive, March 17, 2018, https://nsarchive.gwu.edu/briefing-book/iran/2018-03-07/new-findings-clerical-involvement-1953-coup-iran.
4 "300 Die in Iranian Coup; Shah's Forces Oust Mossadegh," *Chicago Tribune*, August 20, 1953; Kennett Love, "Army Seizes Helm: Ex-Premier and Cabinet Flee Mobs," *New York Times*, August 20, 1953.
5 "New Findings on Clerical Involvement," and Bethany Allen Ebrahimian, "64 Years Later, CIA Finally Releases Details of Iranian Coup," *Foreign Policy*, June 20, 2017.
6 "300 Die in Iran Change of Power: Mossadegh Flees," *Los Angeles Times*, August 20, 1953; "The Important Role of Weeping in Iran's Domestic, Foreign Policy," *Radio Free Europe/Radio Liberty*, September 3, 2010, https://www.rferl.org/a/The_Important_Role_Of_Weeping_In_Irans_Domestic_Foreign_Policy/2147616.html.
7 Kennett Love, "Army Seize Helm: Ex-Premier and Cabinet Flee Mobs," *New York Times*, August 20, 1953.
8 "300 Die in Iranian Coup."
9 Jean-Charles Briton, *US Officials and the Fall of the Shah: Some Safe Contraction Interpretations* (Lanham, MD: Lexington Books, 2010), 34.

10  "Foreign Relations of the United States, 1964–1968, Volume XXII,
    Iran," Office of the Historian, accessed September 13, 2022, https://
    history.state.gov/historicaldocuments/frus1964-68v22/summary.
    "SAVAK" is the abbreviation for Sazman-e Etelaat Va Amniat Keshvar
    (Organization of Intelligence and Security of the Country).
11  Ervand Abrahamian, *Iran between Two Revolutions* (Princeton, NJ:
    Princeton University Press, 1982), 419.
12  Ervand Abrahamian, *A History of Modern Iran* (Cambridge: Cambridge
    University Press, 2008), 125–126.
13  Frances FitzGerald, "Giving the Shah Everything He Wants," *Harper's
    Monthly*, November 1974, 55–84, cited in Abrahamian, *History of
    Modern Iran*, 126.
14  Hedrick Smith, "US Officials Fearful That Shah May Lose Control,"
    *New York Times*, November 6, 1978.
15  Michael Axworthy, *Revolutionary Iran: A History of the Islamic Republic*
    (New York: Oxford University Press, 2013), 108.
16  Axworthy, 112.
17  Axworthy, 113.
18  Axworthy, 126.
19  For a full account, see Axworthy, 145–147; and Christian Caryl, *Strange
    Rebels: 1979 and the Birth of the 21st Century* (New York: Basic Books,
    2013), 143.
20  See, for example, Axworthy, *Revolutionary Iran*, 99.
21  "Iranian Protesters Arrested," *Washington Post*, November 1, 1978.
22  "2,000 in San Francisco in Protest against Shah," *New York Times*,
    December 29, 1978.
23  Robert Lindsey, "Iranian Students Riot in California as Shah's Mother
    Visits," *New York Times*, January 3, 1979; "Shah Sister's Home Stormed:
    Tear Gas Fired in Beverly Hills," *Los Angeles Times*, January 2, 1979.
24  J. Edgar Hoover, "SAC Letter No. 62–20," April 3, 1962, Mary Ferrell
    Foundation, https://www.maryferrell.org/showDoc.html?docId
    =198272#relPageId=1253&search=%22possible_threats%20to%20
    the%20Shah%20or%20his%20party%22.
25  Hoover, "SAC Letter No. 62–20."
26  "Report of Daniel A. Flynn, [FBI] Office: New York, Title: Susan
    Heiligman Frank," March 1, 1968, Mary Ferrell Foundation, https://
    www.maryferrell.org/showDoc.html?docId=120013#relPageId
    =8&search=Hatemi_%22Susan%20Frank%22.
27  "Report of Daniel A. Flynn."
28  "Report of V. Steward Daly, [FBI] Office: San Francisco, California,
    Title: Alleged Illegal Activities of Iranian National Security and
    Intelligence Organization (SAVAK) in the United States," April 22,
    1977, Mary Ferrell Foundation, https://www.maryferrell.org/showDoc
    .html?docId=164057#relPageId=40&search=SAVAK_V.%20Stewart.

29 "Report of V. Steward Daly."
30 Christopher Dickey and Paul W. Valentine, "Iranian Students Disrupt Traffic, Shout Their Way through Downtown," *Washington Post*, November 14, 1978.
31 "444 Days in Tehran: The Story of CIA Officers Held Captive during the Iranian Hostage Crisis," CIA.gov, November 4, 2014, https://www.cia.gov/stories/story/444-days-in-tehran-the-story-of-cia-officers-held-captive-during-the-iranian-hostage-crisis/.
32 Axworthy, *Revolutionary Iran*, 168.
33 "Paul Henze Memo to Zbigniew Brzezinski, 'Thoughts on Iran,'" Confidential, November 9, 1979, National Security Archive, https://nsarchive.gwu.edu/document/19704-national-security-archive-doc-05-paul-henze-memo.
34 "Paul Henze Memo to Zbigniew Brzezinski."
35 "Backlash across US," *Chicago Tribune*, November 9, 1979.
36 "Backlash across US."
37 "A Backlash in America," *Washington Post*, November 8, 1979.
38 Felicity Barringer, "Marching Iranians Cursed, Pelted Here: Iranian Marchers Stir Angry Counterprotest," *Washington Post*, November 10, 1979.
39 Wilber, *Clandestine Service History*, 196.

## Chapter 3   From Harrisburg to Sverdlovsk

Epigraph: Mike Gray and Ira Rosen, *The Warning: Accident at Three Mile Island* (New York: W. W. Norton, 1982), 252.

1 "Three Mile Island Accident," World Nuclear Association, April 2022, https://world-nuclear.org/information-library/safety-and-security/safety-of-plants/three-mile-island-accident.aspx.
2 Donald Janson, "Radiation Is Released in Accident at Nuclear Plant in Pennsylvania," *New York Times*, March 29, 1979.
3 Erin Blakemore, "How the Three Mile Island Accident Was Made Even Worse by the Chaotic Response," *History.com*, March 27, 2019, https://www.history.com/news/three-mile-island-evacuation-orders-controversy.
4 "Backgrounder on the Three Mile Island Accident," U.S. Nuclear Regulatory Commission, accessed June 17, 2022, https://www.nrc.gov/reading-rm/doc-collections/fact-sheets/3mile-isle.html; Tim Selway, "Disaster Averted: Three Mile Island," Pennsylvania Center for the Book, accessed June 17, 2022, https://pabook.libraries.psu.edu/literary-cultural-heritage-map-pa/feature-articles/disaster-averted-three-mile-island.
5 "Radiation Sickness," Mayo Clinic, accessed June 21, 2022, https://www.mayoclinic.org/diseases-conditions/radiation-sickness/symptoms-causes/syc-20377058; "Lethal Dose (LD)," Nuclear Regulatory

Commission, accessed June 21, 2022, https://www.nrc.gov/reading-rm /basic-ref/glossary/lethal-dose-ld.html.

6  George F. Will, "A Film about Greed," *Newsweek*, April 2, 1979, quoted in Gray and Rosen, *The Warning*, 143.

7  Peter Behr, "Three Mile Island Still Haunts U.S. Nuclear Industry," *New York Times*, March 27, 2009. For a comprehensive account of James Creswell's role in sounding the alarm on safety, see Gray and Rosen, *Warning*.

8  John Rockwell, "Rock Stars Are into Politics Again," *New York Times*, September 16, 1979.

9  Carly Simon, "Takin' It to the Streets—No Nukes (MUSE) Concert," YouTube video, September 9, 2012, https://www.youtube.com/watch?v =5maeA8bQh6E.

10  Robert Palmer, "Pop Music: Antinuclear Marathon at Garden," *New York Times*, September 21, 1979.

11  John Rockwell, "Springsteen Makes Biggest Impact at Antinuclear Benefit," *New York Times*, September 24, 1979; Bruce Springsteen, "The River (The River Tour, Tempe 1980)," YouTube video, November 17, 2015, https://www.youtube.com/watch?v=lc6F47Z6PI4.

12  The logic of SALT I was that the greater number of ABM sites, the greater likelihood a country could withstand a nuclear attack, and thus more freely consider using nuclear weapons against its adversary. As such the treaty limited strategic missile defenses to two hundred interceptors each and allowed each side to construct only two defense sites, one to protect the national capital, and the other to protect an ICBM field. "Strategic Arms Limitations Talks/Treaty (SALT) I and II," Office of the Historian, accessed June 11, 2022, https://history.state .gov/milestones/1969-1976/salt.

13  "How Destructive Are Today's Nuclear Weapons?," International Campaign to Abolish Nuclear Weapons, accessed June 11, 2022, https:// www.icanw.org/how_destructive_are_today_s_nuclear_weapons#.

14  SALT I also set limits on how many other offensive missiles each country could retain. For the United States, that would be 1,710 land-based and submarine-based missiles, while the Soviets could retain 2,358. "Strategic Arms Limitations Talks/Treaty (SALT) I and II."

15  "Strategic Arms Limitations Talks/Treaty (SALT) I and II."

16  Raymond Coffey, "Carter Plea for SALT II," *Chicago Tribune*, June 19, 1979.

17  Kevin Klose, "Gromyko Warns Senate against Revising SALT II," *Washington Post*, June 26, 1979.

18  David Hoffman, "Reagan Calls SALT II Dead," *Washington Post*, June 13, 1986.

19  Walter Pincus, "Neutron Killer Warhead Buried in ERDA Budget," *Washington Post*, June 6, 1977.

20 John T. Correll, "The Neutron Bomb," *Air Force Magazine*, October 30, 2017, https://www.airforcemag.com/article/the-neutron-bomb/.

21 "The Peacekeeper [MX] Missile," National Parks Service, accessed September 16, 2022, https://www.nps.gov/articles/mx-peacekeeper-icbm .htm; Wade Boese, "United States Retires MX Missile," Arms Control Association, accessed March 13, 2023, https://www.armscontrol.org/act /2005-10/united-states-retires-mx-missile.

22 Jimmy Carter, "Executive Order 12148—Federal Emergency Management," July 20, 1979, American Presidency Project, https://www .presidency.ucsb.edu/documents/executive-order-12148-federal -emergency-management.

23 "Nominations—DOT & FEMA," Committee of Commerce, Science and Transportation, U.S. Senate, Ninety-Sixth Congress, First Session, December 11, 1979, 36.

24 Nathan Miller, "Both Parties Hail Nixon Decision," *Baltimore Sun*, November 26, 1969; "Text of Nixon Statement on Chemical and Biological War, of the Geneva Protocol and of British Plan," *New York Times*, November 26, 1969; James M. Naughton, "Nixon Renounces Germ Weapons, Orders Destruction of Stocks, Restricts Use of Chemical Arms," *New York Times*, November 26, 1969.

25 With chemical weapons, the United States was only giving up BZ gas, which according to the *New York Times* was expensive, costing $20 a pound, and it took ten tons of it to "knock out a military battalion." Further, its effects were not particularly impressive: "While it makes some people passive, it may make others fly off the handle; in addition, it can, in certain cases, kill its victims." Robert M. Smith, "Germ War: What Nixon Gave Up: Forsworn Weapons Called Probably Unusable," *New York Times*, November 26, 1969.

26 Smith, "Germ War."

27 William Safire, "On Language; Weapons of Mass Destruction," *New York Times*, April 19, 1998.

28 "Britain to Ratify Germ Warfare Ban," *Los Angeles Times*, March 12, 1975.

29 David E. Hoffman, *The Dead Hand: The Untold Story of the Cold War Arms Race and Its Dangerous Legacy* (New York: Anchor Books, 2009), 3; Philip J. Hilts, "US and Russian Doctors Tie Anthrax to Soviets," *New York Times*, March 15, 1993.

30 Tom Mangold and Jeff Goldberg, *Plague Wars: The Terrifying Reality of Biological Warfare* (New York: St. Martin's Press, 2000), 68.

31 "History of Anthrax," Centers for Disease Control, accessed September 17, 2022, https://www.cdc.gov/anthrax/basics/anthrax-history.html.

32 Josh Davis, "The US Military Once Tested Biological Warfare on the Whole of San Francisco," *IFLScience*, July 14, 2015, https://www .iflscience.com/us-military-simulated-biological-warfare-san-francisco -29402; "Secret Testing in the United States," *American Experience*,

accessed September 18, 2022, https://www.pbs.org/wgbh/american experience/features/weapon-secret-testing/.

33 Hoffman, *Dead Hand*, 5.

34 Hilts, "US and Russian Doctors Tie Anthrax to Soviets."

35 Mangold and Goldberg, *Plague Wars*, 68.

36 Mangold and Goldberg, 69.

## Chapter 4    Economic Dislocations

Epigraph: The full quote from Volcker reads: "I would point out that productivity growth in this country is actually negative in a recent period, and we have had higher oil prices. And of course, we import 50% of our oil so that the higher revenues going abroad do not go to American citizens. Under those conditions, the standard of living of the average American has to decline." Some argue that in only citing Volcker's conclusion—which many media outlets did—his meaning was distorted. However, the spirit of the quote, to say nothing of the development of the economy, speaks for itself. "Volcker: 'Standard of Living Has to Decline,'" *Wall Street Journal*, October 29, 1979.

1 "Suicide's Insurance Saves His Company," *New York Times*, February 25, 1960.

2 "Nixon Ends Convertibility of U.S. Dollars to Gold and Announces Wage/Price Controls," August 1971, Federal Reserve History, https:// www.federalreservehistory.org/essays/gold-convertibility-ends; Nick Lioudis, "What Is the Gold Standard? Advantages, Alternatives, and History," *Investopedia*, updated March 4, 2022, https://www.investopedia .com/ask/answers/09/gold-standard.asp.

3 "Nixon and the End of the Bretton Woods System, 1971–1973," Office of the Historian, U.S. Department of State, accessed March 14, 2023, https://history.state.gov/milestones/1969-1976/nixon-shock.

4 "Nixon Ends Convertibility."

5 John Finney, "Nixon Asks $2.2 Billion in Emergency Aid for Israel," *New York Times*, October 20, 1973.

6 Reis Thebault, "Long Lines, High Prices and Fisticuffs: The 1970s Gas Shortages Fueled Bedlam in America," *Washington Post*, May 13, 2021.

7 Thomas Bortelsmann, *The 1970s: A New Global History, from Civil Rights to Economic Inequality* (Princeton, NJ: Princeton University Press, 2012), 137.

8 The emphasis in this chapter on the effects of deindustrialization flows from assumptions on the critical importance of manufacturing in overall social-economic health. In that regard, the work of David Harvey, to say nothing of Karl Marx, is illuminating. See, for example, David Harvey, *A Companion to Marx's Capital* (London: Verso Books,

2010); David Harvey, *A Brief History of Neoliberalism* (Oxford: Oxford University Press, 2005); and Karl Marx, *Capital: A Critique of Political Economy*, vol. 1 (Moscow: Progress Publishers, 1887), in Marxists Internet Archive (hereafter, MIA), https://www.marxists.org/archive/marx/works/1867-c1/.

9  China would eventually become the world's pre-eminent home of manufacturing. As of 2016, 28 percent of China's jobs were in manufacturing. Yi Wen, "China's Rapid Rise: From Backward Agrarian Society to Industrial Powerhouse in Just 35 Years," Federal Reserve Bank of St. Louis, April 11, 2016, https://www.stlouisfed.org/publications/regional-economist/april-2016/chinas-rapid-rise-from-backward-agrarian-society-to-industrial-powerhouse-in-just-35-years; "Distribution of the Workforce across Economic Sectors in China from 2011 to 2021," Statisa, accessed August 23, 2002, http://www.crosscurrents.hawaii.edu/content.aspx?lang=eng&site=japan&theme=work&subtheme=INDUS&unit=JWORK063.

10  See Peter Cheney, "The Rise of Japan: How the Car Industry Was Won," *Globe & Mail*, November 5, 2015; Ingo Koehler, "Overcoming Stagnation: Product Policy and Marketing in the German Automobile Industry of the 1970s," *Business History Review* 84, no. 1 (Spring 2010): 53–78; and "The Japanese Electronics Industry," *Cross Currents*, accessed October 13, 2023, http://www.crosscurrents.hawaii.edu/content.aspx?lang=eng&site=japan&theme=work&subtheme=INDUS&unit=JWORK063.

11  William Robbins, "Philadelphia Suffers in Manufacturing Job Exodus," *New York Times*, August 15, 1981.

12  "New York's Decline in Manufacturing Gains Momentum in 1980," *New York Times*, March 22, 1981.

13  While a fuller examination of the relationship between crime and deindustrialization is beyond this work, a few points are worth noting. Between 1960 and 1970 violent crime in the United States increased by 126 percent, and by another 64 percent between 1970 and 1980. Lauren Brook Eisen, "America's Faulty Perception of Crime Rates," Brennan Center, March 16, 2015, https://www.brennancenter.org/our-work/analysis-opinion/americas-faulty-perception-crime-rates. Also, Garland White reports a correlation between crime and the loss of manufacturing: "The correlations throughout suggest that the loss of jobs is tied most significantly to crime rates. The indicators of industrial decline are correlated with drug arrests. Together, the decline in manufacturing and the increases in unemployment account for a significant increase in rates for burglaries, drug offenses, and robberies when other relevant variables are controlled. We also find a consistent relationship between cities' losses of industrial jobs and increases in aggravated assaults." Garland White, "Crime and the Decline of Manufacturing, 1970–1990," *Justice Quarterly* 16, no. 1, 94: x.

14  "Plant Closings and Relocations," Committee on Labor and Relations, U.S. Senate, Ninety-Sixth Congress, First Session, January 22, 1979, 59.

15  "Plant Closings and Relocations," 61.

16  Douglas R. Sease, "U.S. Steel Is Set to Close Over 12 of Its Facilities," *Wall Street Journal*, November 28, 1979.

17  "American Nightmare Comes True," *Guardian*, December 12, 1979.

18  James L. Rowe Jr., "Imports, Modernization: Dealing with Old Steel Problems in Crisis Atmosphere," *Washington Post*, October 16, 1977.

19  "American Nightmare Comes True."

20  "American Nightmare Comes True."

21  Doug Smith, "Furnaces at U.S. Steel Burn Out for Last Time," *Los Angeles Times*, December 27, 1979.

22  Smith, "Furnaces at U.S. Steel Burn Out for Last Time."

23  "American Nightmare Comes True."

24  Staughton Lynd, "Reindustrialization: Brownfield or Greenfield?," *Democracy: A Journal of Political Renewal and Radial Change* 1, no. 3 (July 1981): 25.

25  As of 2021, there were seventeen thousand people working in coal mining in West Virginia, the lowest number since 1890. "West Virginia Coal Mine Jobs in 2021 Were Fewest since 1890," *West Virginia Public Broadcasting*, May 2, 2022, https://wvpublic.org/west-virginia-coal -mine-jobs-in-2021-were-fewest-since-1890/.

26  "A Short History of Mining—and Its Decline—in West Virginia," *Register Herald*, March 30, 2017, https://www.register-herald.com /opinion/columns/a-short-history-of-mining—and-its-decline—in /article_4c968cfd-8d8b-51c7-bccb-77e186ea61f7.html.

27  Devashree Saha and Sifan Liu, "Increased Automation Guarantees Bleak Outlook for Trump's Promises," Brookings Institute, January 25, 2017, https://www.brookings.edu/blog/the-avenue/2017/01/25/automation -guarantees-a-bleak-outlook-for-trumps-promises-to-coal-miners/.

28  "The History of Word Processing," Templafy, December 11, 2018, https://www.templafy.com/blog/the-history-of-word-processing/; Greg Daugherty, "The Rise and Fall of Telephone Operators," *History.com*, August 2, 2021, https://www.history.com/news/rise-fall-telephone -switchboard-operators; "Telephone Operators," *Engineering and Technology Wiki*, accessed April 9, 2023, https://ethw.org/Telephone _Operators.

29  Margaret Thatcher, "Speech to Small Business Bureau Conference," February 8, 1984, Margaret Thatcher Foundation, https://www .margaretthatcher.org/document/105617.

30  Thatcher, "Speech to Small Business Bureau Conference."

31  Ronald Regan, "Inaugural Address 1981," January 20, 1981, Ronald Reagan Presidential Library and Museum, https://www.reaganlibrary .gov/archives/speech/inaugural-address-1981.

32  Harvey, *Brief History of Neoliberalism*, 2.
33  "Statement of Aims," Mont Pelerin Society, accessed September 29, 2022, https://www.montpelerin.org/event/429dba23-fc64-4838-aea3 -b847011022a4/websitePage:6950c74b-5d9b-41cc-8da1-3e1991c14ac5.
34  Reginald Stuart, "Chryslers Records 1.1 Billion '79 Loss, Believed a Record," *New York Times*, February 8, 1980.
35  Ira R. Allen, "Chrysler Bailout: Backroom Drama," *Chicago Tribune*, December 30, 1979; Levin Welch, "Neoliberalism, Economic Crisis, and the 2008 Financial Meltdown in the United States," *International Review of Modern Sociology* 38, no. 2 (Autumn 2012): 252.
36  "Volcker's Announcement of Anti-Inflation Measures," October 1979, Federal Reserve History, https://www.federalreservehistory.org/essays /anti-inflation-measures.
37  Nicholas Kristoff, "We're No. 28 and Dropping," *New York Times*, September 9, 2020.
38  Nancy L. Ross, "After 10 Years of Change," *Washington Post*, December 30, 1979.

## Chapter 5   China on the Capitalist Road

Epigraph: "Resolution of C.P.C. Central Committee on Dismissing Deng Xiaoping from All Posts Both inside and outside Party," *Peking Review*, no. 15 (April 9, 1976), in MIA, https://www.marxists.org/subject/china /peking-review/1976/PR1976–15b.htm.
 1  Fredrick C. Teiwes, *The End of the Maoist Era* (Armonk, ME: Sharpe, 2007), 1 and 25.
 2  Chang Chun-Chiao (Zhang Chunqiao), *On Exercising All Around Dicta- torship of the Bourgeoise* (Beijing: Foreign Languages Press, 1975), in MIA, https://www.marxists.org/reference/archive/zhang/1975/x01/x01.htm.
 3  See Teiwes, *End of the Maoist Era*, chap. 7.
 4  Maurice Meisner, *The Deng Xiaoping Era: An Inquiry into the Fate of Chinese Socialism, 1978–1994* (New York: Hill and Wang, 1996), 58.
 5  Meisner, *Deng Xiaoping Era*, 74.
 6  Frederick C. Teiwes, "The Paradoxical Post-Mao Transition: From Obeying the Leader to 'Normal Politics,'" *China Journal*, no. 34 (July 1995): 55–94.
 7  After assuming power over Hua, Deng downplayed the event: "These kinds of changes happen in any country. There is nothing strange about that?" Reuters dispatch on Deng's press conference, *Sydney Morning Herald*, February 14, 1981; see also Teiwes, "Paradoxical Post-Mao Transition."
 8  "Communique of the Third Plenary Session of the 11th Central Com- mittee of The Communist Party of China" (Adopted on December 22, 1978), *Peking Review* 21, no. 52 (December 29, 1978), in MIA, https:// www.marxists.org/subject/china/peking-review/1978/PR1978-52.pdf.

9  "Can an Enterprise Be Run without Rules and Regulations?," *Peking Review* 21, no. 37 (September 15, 1978), in MIA, https://www.marxists .org/subject/china/peking-review/1978/PR1978-37.pdf; "Observe Economic Laws: Speed Up the Four Modernizations," *Peking Review* 21, no. 45 (November 10, 1978), in MIA, https://www.marxists.org/subject /china/peking-review/1978/PR1978-45.pdf.

10  Hua Guofeng, "Speech the National Finance and Trade Conference on Learning from Taching and Tachai," *Peking Review* 21, no. 30 (July 28, 1978), in MIA, https://www.marxists.org/subject/china/peking-review /1978/PR1978-30.pdf.

11  Oriana Fallaci, "Deng: Cleaning Up Mao's 'Feudal Mistakes,'" *Washington Post*, August 31, 1980.

12  Fallaci, "Deng."

13  Meisner, *Deng Xiaoping Era*, 142.

14  "Liberalized Attitudes on Sex Urged by Wall Poster in Peking," *Los Angeles Times*, January 4, 1979.

15  Frank Chin, "China's Wall Posters Are Mostly Creations of Ordinary Citizens," *Wall Steet Journal*, December 1, 1978; John Fraser, "Peking Posters: New Boldness in Talk of Rights: 'Propaganda Teams' Take Message to Main Cities," *Christian Science Monitor*, December 28, 1978.

16  "Peking Poster Criticizes China on Human Rights," *Los Angeles Times*, December 11, 1978.

17  Deng Xiaoping, "Uphold the Four Basic Principles," speech given March 30, 1979, Asia for Educators, Columbia University, http://afe .easia.columbia.edu/ps/cup/deng_xiaoping_uphold_principles.pdf.

18  James P. Sterba, "Peking Closes Democracy Wall, Banishes Posters to Remote Park," *New York Times*, December 7, 1979.

19  "Implementing the Socialist Principle 'To Each according to His Work,'" *Peking Review* 21, no. 31 (August 4, 1978), in MIA, https://www .marxists.org/subject/china/peking-review/1978/PR1978-31.pdf.

20  Karl Marx, *Critique of the Gotha Programme* (written 1875), in MIA, https://www.marxists.org/archive/marx/works/1875/gotha/index.htm.

21  Linda Matthews, "A New Leap: Modernizing China: Teng's Daring Drive," *Los Angeles Times*, February 8, 1979.

22  Jack Raymond, "US Called Ready to Use Atom Arms," *New York Times*, September 28, 1958.

## Chapter 6  Up against the Wall

Epigraph: "Bob Avakian Speech in Cleveland," *Revolutionary Worker* 1, no. 48 (April 4, 1980), in MIA, https://www.marxists.org/history/erol /periodicals/revolutionary-worker/rw-1-48.pdf.

1  "Eldridge Cleaver Speaking at UCLA, 10/4/1968," UCLACommStud-ies YouTube, 4:55, https://www.youtube.com/watch?v=mfRxv

_Nz4MY; John F. Burns, "Cleaver Seized on Return Here after 7-Year Exile," *New York Times*, November 19, 1975.

2   Mark Stillman, "Eldridge Cleaver's New Pants: Every Revolution Needs a Haberdasher, Right?," *Harvard Crimson*, September 26, 1975; "Eldridge Cleaver Quotation," Roz Payne Sixties Archive, accessed July 20, 2022, https://rozsixties.unl.edu/items/show/567.

3   Jerry Rubin, *Do It! Scenarios of the Revolution* (New York: Simon and Schuster, 1970), 14–15; "The Three Piece Jerry Rubin," *Washington Post*, August 5, 1980; Jerry Rubin, "Guess Who's Coming to Wall Street," *New York Times*, July 30, 1980.

4   Lacey Fosburgh, "Leary Scored as 'Cop Informant' by His Son and 2 Close Friends," *New York Times*, September 19, 1974; "Records: Leary Helped the FBI," *Tampa Bay Times*, July 1, 1999.

5   Mark A. Stein and Valarie Basheda, "Huey Newton Found Shot to Death on Oakland Street: Black Panthers Founder Killed in High Drug Area," *Los Angeles Times*, August 22, 1989.

6   Les Ledbetter, "Huey Newton Seized on Intent to Murder," *New York Times*, May 12, 1978; "Rennie Davis, Antiwar Activist, Now Focuses Life on Guru, 15," *New York Times*, May 6, 1973.

7   FBI report on the Revolutionary Communist Party, Chicago CG 100–56726, September 6, 1976, David Sullivan U.S. Maoism Collection, NYU-TAM.527, Box 23 Folders 5–6.

8   Christopher Dickey and Alfred E. Lewis, "5 Men Arrested after Attack on China Chancery," *Washington Post*, January 25, 1979.

9   "Violence Flares Briefly in Day of Varied Protests," *Washington Post*, January 30, 1979.

10  Paul W. Valentine and B. D. Colen, "D.C. Court Orders $10,00 Bonds on Maoist Rioters," *Washington Post*, January 31, 1979.

11  A sense of its small size can be seen in the group's newspaper, *Workers Viewpoint*, which lists only a P.O. Box in New York as a point of contact, with no information on a national office or specific chapters. See *Workers Viewpoint* 3, no. 9 (September 1978), in MIA, https://www.marxists.org/history/erol/periodicals/workers-viewpoint/wv-3-9.pdf; and *Workers Viewpoint* 5, no. 1 (January 9, 1980), in MIA, https://www.marxists.org/history/erol/periodicals/workers-viewpoint/wv-5-1.pdf.

12  While the name change did not occur till October 1979, for simplicity, unless in quoted text, I refer to the WVO as the CWP.

13  "The Pigs Don't Want the People to Hear It: Greensboro Tour," *Revolutionary Worker* 1, no. 24 (October 19, 1979), in MIA, https://www.marxists.org/history/erol/periodicals/revolutionary-worker/rw-1-24.pdf.

14  Elizabeth Wheaton, *Codename Greenkill: The 1979 Greensboro Killings* (Athens: University of Georgia Press, 1987), 107.

15 *The New Order*, August 1979, reprinted in the *Revolutionary Worker* 1, no. 27 (November 9, 1979), in MIA, https://www.marxists.org/history /erol/periodicals/revolutionary-worker/rw-1-27.pdf.

16 Wheaton, *Codename Greenkill*, 109.

17 Tom Stites, "Four Shot to Death at Anti-Klan March," *New York Times*, November 4, 1979; "Greensboro Truth and Reconciliation Commission Report: Executive Summary," May 25, 2006, DigitalNC, https://lib .digitalnc.org/record/26070?ln=en.

18 *Greensboro: Closer to the Truth*, directed by Adam Zucker (Ann Arbor, MI: Filmmakers Library, 2009).

19 "Turn Grief into Strength! Avenge the CWP 5!," CWP flier, November 1979, Duke University, https://gateway.uncg.edu/islandora/object /duke%3A243#page/1/mode/1up.

20 "4 Slain Communist Activists Buried in Greensboro amid Tight Security," *Baltimore Sun*, November 12, 1979; Howell Raines, "500 March in a Procession for Five Slain Communists," *New York Times*, November 12, 1979; Wheaton, *Codename Greenkill*, 175.

21 "What MOVE Members Insist They Believe In," *Afro-American*, March 18, 1978.

22 Jim Quinn and Ralph Flood, "Philadelphia Escalates Its Conflict with an Anarchist Group," *Washington Post*, March 17, 1978; John L. Puckett and Devin DeSilvis, "MOVE in Powelton Village," West Philadelphia Collaborative History, accessed March 16, 2023, https:// collaborativehistory.gse.upenn.edu/stories/move-powelton-village.

23 Gregory Jaynes, "Officer Killed as Philadelphia Radicals Are Evicted," *New York Times*, August 9, 1978; Murray Dubin, "Move Members Found Guilty of Death of Officer," *Washington Post*, May 9, 1980.

24 Pamela Smith, "Bulldozers Fail to Destroy Spirit of MOVE after Demolishing Compound," *Philadelphia Tribune*, August 11, 1978.

25 Bem A. Franklin, "Verdicts Are Due in 'Move' Killing Trial," *New York Times*, May 6, 1980.

26 Karen De Witt, "Murder Trial of in Radical Group Seen Heating Up," *New York Times*, December 17, 1979; Puckett and DeSilvis, "MOVE in Powelton Village."

27 Both groups in 1979 argued that the potential for a major upsurge awaited in the 1980s. The RCP put forward the slogan "If you liked the '60s, you'll love the '80s," while the CWP predicted the "80's Economic Crisis Will Make the 30's Great Depression Look Like a Picnic." See "What the CWP Is Copying and What It Is Not," *Revolutionary Worker* 2, no. 10 (July 4, 1980), in MIA, https://www.marxists.org /history/erol/periodicals/revolutionary-worker/rw-2-10.pdf; and *Workers Viewpoint* 5, no. 21 (June 16, 1980), in MIA, https://www .marxists.org/history/erol/periodicals/workers-viewpoint/wv-5-21.pdf.

## Chapter 7   The Use of Terrorism

Epigraph: Oversight Hearings before the Subcommittee on Civil and
Constitutional Rights of the Committee on the Judiciary, House of
Representatives, Ninety-Ninth Congress, First and Second Session on
Terrorism, August 26, 1985, and February 28, May 14 and 15, 1986 (hereafter,
Oversight Hearings), Statement of William B. Quandt, the Brookings
Institution, 10.

1   Arthur M. Eckstein, *Bad Moon Rising: How the Weathermen Beat the
    FBI and Lost the Revolution* (New Haven, CT: Yale University Press,
    2016), 11–13.

2   Lawrence Roberts, *May Day 1971: A White House at War, a Revolt in the
    Streets, and the Untold History of America's Biggest Mass Arrest* (Boston:
    Mariner Books, 2020), 4–6; Philip Bump, "A History of Attacks on the
    U.S. Capitol, 44 Years after the Weather Underground Bombing,"
    *Washington Post*, March 2, 2015.

3   R. L Shackelford to E. S. Miller, Re: WEATHFUG, May 8, 1972,
    Mark W. Felt FBI file, Section 9, Archive.org, pdf, 163–164 (hereafter
    Felt FBI file, Section 9), https://ia801509.us.archive.org/26/items
    /MarkFelt/1104977-001%20---%2062-HQ-118045%20---%20Sec-
    tion%209%20(867521).pdf. Those small numbers are in sync with author
    Bryan Burrough's assessment. As he reports, "One estimate puts
    thirty-five people underground during the 1972–73 time frame a count
    endorsed by several alumni." Bryan Burrough, *Days of Rage: America's
    Radical Underground, the FBI and the Forgotten Age of Revolutionary
    Violence* (New York: Penguin, 2015), 218.

4   John Kiffner, "Rudd in Surrender; Freed Pending Trial," *New York
    Times*, September 9, 1977.

5   Burrough, *Days of Rage*, 79.

6   Weather Underground, *Prairie Fire: The Politics of Revolutionary
    Anti-Imperialism*, Communications Co. 1974, 1 (ellipses in original).

7   Farr, "Four Plead Guilty in Briggs Bombing Plot," *Los Angeles Times*,
    December 28, 1978; Bill Farr, "Man Sentenced in Briggs Bomb Plot,"
    *Los Angeles Times*, June 30, 1979.

8   Marcella S. Kreiter, "Former Radical Leader Bernadine Dohrn
    Surrenders to Authorities Wednesday," United Press International,
    December 3, 1980; Paul Montgomery, "Last of Radical Leaders Eluded
    Police for 11 Years," *New York Times*, October 25, 1981.

9   For more on BLA and RNA members, see Edward Onaci, *Free the
    Land: The Republic of New Afrika and the Pursuit of a Black Nation-
    State* (Chapel Hill: University of North Carolina Press, 2020),
    158–183.

10  See, for example, Flores Forbes, *Will You Die with Me? My Life and the
    Black Panther Party* (New York: Atria Books, 2010); and Sean L. Malloy,

"Uptight in Babylon: Eldridge Cleaver's Cold War," *Diplomatic History* 37, no. 3 (June 2013): 538–571.

11 After spending nineteen years in jail, Bin Wahad was released after proving prosecutors withheld evidence that could have led to his acquittal. See *The People of the State of New York, Plaintiff, v. Dhoruba Bin Wahad, Formerly Known as Richard Moore, Defendant*, Supreme Court, New York County, January 7, 1993, Leagle, https://www.leagle.com/decision/1993559154misc2d4051490.

12 Edith Evans Asbury, "13 Panthers Here Found Not Guilty on All 12 Counts," *New York Times*, May 14, 1971; Edith Evans Asbury, "Detective Tells Panther Trial of His Attempt to Save Malcolm," *New York Times*, December 8, 1970; Frank Donner, *Protectors of the Privilege: Red Squads and Police Repression in Urban America* (Berkeley: University of California Press, 1990), 182–183, and 187–190; Christopher Rhodes, "Looking Back at the 'Panther 21' Trial, 50 Years Later," *Blavity*, May 10, 2021, https://blavity.com/looking-back-at-the-panther-21-trial-50-years-later?category1=news&category2=politics.

13 Joseph F. Sullivan, "Panther, Trooper Slain in Shoot-Out," *New York Times*, May 3, 1973.

14 Andrew Cooper, "Street Rumor: Chesimard May Not Be Taken Alive: Joanne Chesimard Believed to Be in NYC," *Amsterdam News*, November 10, 1979; Robert Hanley, "No Checking Was Done on Chesimard 'Visitors': Identification Required of Visitors Security Review," *New York Times*, November 6, 1979; Burrough, *Days of Rage*, 476–479.

15 Arnold H. Lubasch, "Killer Says He Helped in Chesimard's Escape," *New York Times*, December 2, 1987; Arnold H. Lubasch, "Brink's Testimony Examining Escape," *New York Times*, May 15, 1983.

16 "Joint Terrorism Task Forces," FBI.gov, accessed July 24, 2022, https://www.fbi.gov/investigate/terrorism/joint-terrorism-task-forces.

17 Oversight Hearings, Statement of Lt. Kevin Hallinan, 235.

18 Oversight Hearings, 173–174.

19 Michael Getler, "Haig Escapes Apparent Try on His Life," *Washington Post*, June 26, 1979; "German Terrorist Convicted of Attempt on Alexander Haig," Associated Press, July 3, 1991.

20 Paddy Clancy, "Lord Mountbatten's Assassination by the IRA," British Heritage, August 18, 2023, https://britishheritage.com/history/lord-mountbatten-death.

## Chapter 8   The FBI, beyond Reform

Epigraph: "W. Mark Felt Interview," August 29, 1976, *C-SPAN*, https://www.c-span.org/video/?187059-1/w-mark-felt-interview. The interview was originally broadcast as an episode of the CBS news program *Face the Nation*; this quote appears at 7:50.

1  Jeffrey Brown, "How Actress Jean Seberg Became a Target of the FBI," *PBS News Hour*, February 26, 2020, https://www.pbs.org/newshour /show/american-actress-jean-seberg-supported-the-black-panthers-did-it -cost-her-career. For a full account of COINTELPRO operations, see *Supplementary Detailed Staff Reports on Intelligence Activities and the Rights of Americans, Book III, Final Report of the Select Committee to Study Governmental Operation with Respect to Intelligence Activities* (Washington, DC: U.S. Government Printing Office, 1976) (hereafter, Church Committee Report).

2  "I'm the Guy They Called Deep Throat," *Vanity Fair*, July 2005.

3  See, for example, Tim Weiner, "W. Mark Felt, Watergate Deep Throat, Dies at 95," *New York Times*, December 19, 2008.

4  John A. Crewdson and Nicholas M. Horroch, "F.B.I. Reportedly Stole Mail in Its Drive on War Foes," *New York Times*, August 8, 1976.

5  "W. Mark Felt Interview," opening statement.

6  "W. Mark Felt Interview," 16:00.

7  "W. Mark Felt Interview," 9:00.

8  See Church Committee Report.

9  The CPUSA COINTELPRO operations constituted 1,388 of the total 2,370 (Church Committee Report, 58).

10  While some of the documents relating to the CPUSA COINTELPRO operations have been released, many have not. A case in point is the Bureau's file on its Ad Hoc Committee (AHC) for a Marxist-Leninist Party, numbering over fifteen thousand pages. The AHC was a program the FBI developed to disrupt the CPUSA. A nominally Maoist group, it actually consisted of FBI informants. See Aaron J. Leonard and Conor A. Gallagher, *A Threat of the First Magnitude* (London: Repeater Books, 2017), chap. 1; and Aaron J. Leonard and Conor A. Gallagher, *Heavy Radicals* (Winchester, UK: Zero Books, 2022), xv–xix.

11  Childs would continue to provide information until 1981. For more, see John Barron, *Operation Solo: The FBI's Man in the Kremlin* (Washington, DC: Regnery Publishing, 2013); David Garrow, *The FBI and Martin Luther King, Jr.: From Solo to Memphis* (New York: W. W. Norton, 1981); and Leonard and Gallagher, *Threat of the First Magnitude*, chap. 2.

12  Leonard and Gallagher, *Heavy Radicals*, intro.

13  Leonard and Gallagher, *Heavy Radicals*, 122–124.

14  Testimony of David Ryan, Criminal Case File 78–00179, *United States v. W. Mark Felt and Edward S. Miller*, NARA Stacks: 16W3/15/05/05-06, Box 30, 3963, Records of the District Courts of the United States, District of Columbia, Record Group 21, National Archives, Washington, DC (hereafter, "Record Group 21, Felt and Miller").

15  David Wise, "The FBI Pardoned," *New York Times*, April 28, 1981.

16 E. S. Miller to Mr. Felt, "Re: U.S. China Friendship Association," April 17, 1973, (Felt FBI file, Section 9, 82).

17 Record Group 21, Felt and Miller, 4003.

18 FBI, *The Federal Bureau of Investigation's Compliance with the Attorney General's Investigative Guidelines (Redacted)*, Special Report, September 2005, Office of the Inspector General, https://oig.justice.gov/sites /default/files/archive/special/0509/chapter2.htm, chap. 2.

19 FBI, *Federal Bureau of Investigation's Compliance*.

20 See Barron, *Operation Solo*, and the Operation SOLO files published by the FBI online: "SOLO," The Vault, accessed October 23, 2022, https://vault.fbi.gov/solo?b_start:int=120.

21 "W. Mark Felt Interview," 8:39.

22 "About the Foreign Intelligence Surveillance Court," United States Foreign Intelligence Surveillance Court, accessed October 5, 2022, https://www.fisc.uscourts.gov/about-foreign-intelligence-surveillance -court; David Kris, "How the FISA Court Really Works," Lawfare, September 2, 2018, https://www.lawfareblog.com/how-fisa-court-really -works.

23 "The Foreign Intelligence Surveillance Act of 1978 (FISA)," Bureau of Justice Assistance, https://bja.ojp.gov/program/it/privacy-civil-liberties /authorities/statutes/1286.

24 Benjamin Civiletti, Attorney General, to Vice President, U.S. Senate, Re: FISA Report 1978, Federation of American Scientists, https://irp.fas .org/agency/doj/fisa/1979rept.html.

25 Aaron J. Leonard and Conor A. Gallagher, "Newly Obtained FBI Files Shed New Light on the Murder of Fred Hampton," *Jacobin*, March 2, 2021; Aaron J. Leonard and Conor A. Gallagher, "We Obtained New FBI Documents on How and Why Fred Hampton Was Murdered," *Jacobin*, March 31, 2021 (hereafter, "Leonard and Gallagher, *Jacobin* articles").

26 "J. Edgar Hoover: Panthers Greatest Threat to US Security," United Press International, July 16, 1969, accessed December 10, 2022, https:// www.upi.com/Archives/1969/07/16/J-Edgar-Hoover-Black-Panther -Greatest-Threat-to-US-Security/1571551977068/, the section of the annual report Hoover was publicizing, "Protecting Our Internal Security," opens by discussing the New Left, *before* moving to Black extremists. *FBI Annual Report, Fiscal Year 1969* (Washington, DC: FBI), 21–23, archive.org, https://archive.org/details /fbiannualreport1969_202001.

27 Joshua Bloom and Waldo S. Martin, in the introduction to their definitive political history of the BPP quote Hoover saying "The Black Panther party, without question, represents the greatest threat to the internal security of the country"—leaving out the contextualization. Later in the text they repeat the quote, though properly contextualized. That mention

is in turn accompanied by an extensive footnote that attempts to chase down Hoover's remarks beyond the UPI story, but concludes, "To date we have not been able to recover the precise context of the quote, but at least the UPI stories [*sic*] date it precisely." Given such a thin foundation, it is a wonder the mischaracterization of Hoover's remarks has gained the currency it has. Joshua Bloom and Waldo E. Martin, *Black Against Empire: The History and Politics of the Black Panther Party*, (Berkeley, University of California Press, 2013), 3, 210, and 445.

28  David Young, "Panther Tip on 'Hit Squad': Informer aids FBI in quiz," *Chicago Tribune*, February 3, 1973.

29  "Interview with William O'Neal," April 13, 1989, Washington University in St Louis Digital Gateway, http://repository.wustl.edu/concern /videos/0r96776r1n.

30  Leonard and Gallagher, *Jacobin* articles.

31  SAC Chicago to Director, FBI, Subject: [REDACTED], April 16, 1969, in Roy Martin Mitchell FBI personnel file, second FOIA release to author, February 27, 2023, CD/pdf, 154–155. (Hereafter Mitchell, II).

32  Leonard and Gallagher, *Jacobin* articles.

33  Robert Mitchell, "The Police Raid That Killed Two Black Panthers, Shook Chicago and Changed the Nation," *Washington Post*, December 4, 2019, https://www.washingtonpost.com/history/2019/12/04/police-raid -that-left-two-black-panthers-dead-shook-chicago-changed-nation/.

34  Nathaniel Sheperd, "Plaintiffs in Panthers Suit 'Knew We Were Right,'" *New York Times*, November 14, 1982; *Hampton v. Hanrahan*, U.S. Court of Appeals, Seventh Circuit, April 23, 1979, Casetext, https:// casetext.com/case/hampton-v-hanrahan.

35  Young, "Panther Tip on 'Hit Squad.'"

36  "Court Won't Review Murder-for-Hire Case," United Press International, October 1, 1984.

37  J. Edgar Hoover to Roy Martin Mitchell, December 10, 1969, in Mitchell FBI personnel file.

38  "*Beard v. Mitchell*, No. 78–2592. Argued April 27, 1979. Decided August 7, 1979. Rehearing and Rehearing in Banc Denied October 19, 1979," Casetext, accessed October 3, 2022, https://casetext.com/case /beard-v-mitchell.

39  William A. Webster to Thomas P. Sullivan, January 19, 1979, in Mitchell FBI personnel file. Routing instructions on the bottom of the letter read "Personal Attention SAC: Bring to the attention of SA Roy Martin Mitchell."

40  Webster to Sullivan.

41  Roy Martin Mitchell, Personnel Summary, September 1973, 9–10, Mitchell II, CD/pdf, 69–70.

42  Mitchell, II, 69–70.

43  Mitchell, II, 69–70.

44 Mitchell, II, 69–70.
45 *Beard v. Mitchell.*
46 Maurice Possley, "FBI Informant Cleared in Murder by Cop," *Chicago Tribune*, February 28, 1984.
47 Possley, "FBI Informant Cleared in Murder by Cop."
48 Ronald Reagan, "Statement on Granting Pardons to W. Mark Felt and Edward S. Miller," April 15, 1981, Ronald Reagan Presidential Library and Museum, https://www.reaganlibrary.gov/archives/speech/statement-granting-pardons-w-mark-felt-and-edward-s-miller-0.

## Chapter 9    After Disco

Epigraph: Mick Jones quoted in Marc Myers, "The Sound of Going to Pieces: The Clash's Surviving Members Recount the Making of a Punk Anthem," *Wall Street Journal*, August 29, 2013.
1 Richard Dozer, "Sox Promotion Ends in a Mob Scene," *Chicago Tribune*, July 13, 1979.
2 Gary Deeb, "Steve Dahl: The DJ Who Rocked the Sox—and Started All That Talk," *Chicago Tribune*, July 16, 1979.
3 Dave Marsh, "The Flip Side of '79," *Rolling Stone*, December 22, 1979.
4 Eric Siegel, "What Is It about Disco That Kindles Such Rage?," *Baltimore Sun*, July 22, 1979.
5 Alex Brummer, "Drugs a Cause of Panic Which Killed Who Fans," *Guardian*, December 5, 1979.
6 "Rock Fans Stampede; 11 Trampled to Death," *Chicago Tribune*, December 4, 1979.
7 Robert Mcg. Thomas Jr., "11 Killed and 8 Badly Hurt in Crush before Rock Concert in Cincinnati," *New York Times*, December 4, 1979.
8 "'Please Open the Doors, There Are People Dying out Here,' Bruised Rock Fan Recalls," *Baltimore Sun*, December 5, 1979.
9 Dave Lifton, "How Bruce Springsteen Upped His Game on 'Darkness on the Edge of Town,'" *Ultimate Classic Rock*, June 4, 2013, https://ultimateclassicrock.com/bruce-springsteen-darkness-on-the-edge-of-town/.
10 Robert Hilburn, "Springsteen, the Class of the Field," *Los Angeles Times*, July 7, 1978.
11 See, for example, Jo Durden-Smith, *Who Killed George Jackson* (New York: Knopf, 1976); Gregory Armstrong, *The Dragon Has Come* (New York: Harper Row, 1974); and Mike Kelly, "What Really Happened That Night at the Lafayette Bar and Grill in Paterson?," *NorthJersey.com*, June 17, 2019, https://www.northjersey.com/story/news/columnists/mike-kelly/2019/06/17/rubin-carter-john-artis-what-really-happened-night/1419996001/.
12 Robert Hilburn, "Bob Dylan's Song of Salvation," *Los Angeles Times*, November 24, 1980; "Bob Dylan Gets Religion in the 'Gospel Years,'

Part 2," *Goldmine*, February 23, 2009, https://www.goldminemag.com
/articles/bob-dylan-gets-religion-in-the-gospel-years-part-2.

13  Robert Cross, "The '70s: The Age of Depletion," *Chicago Tribune*,
December 9, 1979.

14  "Eldridge Cleaver Quotation," Roz Paine Sixties Archive, accessed
January 26, 2023, https://rozsixties.unl.edu/items/show/567.

15  Geoffrey Hines, "Self-Righteous Dylan," *Washington Post*, September 19, 1979.

16  Hilburn, "Bob Dylan's Song of Salvation."

17  Dan McGuill, "Did Eric Clapton Once Unleash a Racist Rant
Onstage?," Snopes.com, December 4, 2020, https://www.snopes.com
/fact-check/eric-clapton-racist-rant/; Enoch Powell, speech to the
Conservative Association meeting in Birmingham on April 20, 1968,
*Anthropology 1001* (blog), https://anth1001.files.wordpress.com/2014/04
/enoch-powell_speech.pdf.

18  A good assessment of Clapton in the seventies can be found in "Eric
Clapton: Backless, Hapless and Almost Hopeless," *Washington Post*,
January 3, 1979.

19  Bowie would unequivocally renounce those views. Clapton, while
rejecting his earlier statements, in a 2018 interview offered a defense that
belied a deeper understanding: "Half of my friends were black, I dated a
black woman, and I championed black music." See Jessica Lee, "Did
David Bowie Say He Supports Fascism and Call Hitler a 'Rock Star'?,"
Snopes.com December 23, 2020, https://www.snopes.com/fact-check
/rock-star-david-bowie/; and Tom Sykes, "Eric Clapton Apologizes for
Racist Past: 'I Sabotaged Everything,'" *Daily Beast*, January 12, 2018,
https://www.thedailybeast.com/eric-clapton-apologizes-for-racist-past-i
-sabotaged-everything.

20  RAR had only modest success in the United States holding only small
events in New York's Central Park and Chicago's Lincoln Park. "Rock
Against Racism in Park Today," *New York Times*, May 5, 1979; see also
the RAR flier posted on Wikipedia Commons, accessed November 14,
2022, https://upload.wikimedia.org/wikipedia/commons/0/0a
/Rockaginstracismleaflet.jpg.

21  Robert Hilburn, "Clash: A New Rock Import," *Los Angeles Times*,
February 2, 1979.

22  "10 Times the Clash's 'London Calling' Was Recognized as One of the
Greatest Albums of All Time," Capitol Theater, April 7, 2019, https://
www.thecapitoltheatre.com/blog/detail/10-times-the-clashs-london
-calling-was-recognized-as-one-of-the-greatest-albums-of-all-time.

23  Pat Gilbert, *Passion Is a Fashion: The Real Story of the Clash* (London:
Aurum Press, 2005), 239, 367. For DC-10 crashes see "No Survivors
Found," *New York Times*, May 26, 1979; and "74 Die in DC-10 Crash in
Mexico," *New York Times*, November 1, 1979.

24  Myers, "Sound of Going to Pieces."
25  Timothy White, "The Life and Times of Reggae," *New York Times,* July 22, 1979.
26  "Haile Selassie and Africa," *BBC,* October 21, 2009, https://www.bbc .co.uk/religion/religions/rastafari/beliefs/haileselassie.shtml.
27  White, "Life and Times of Reggae."
28  "Records: Marley and the Wailers: Triumph of Art over Ire," *Los Angeles Times,* April 9, 1978.
29  Robert Hilburn, "Pauley Pavilion Concert: Marley Send His Message through Special Delivery," *Los Angeles Times,* November 27, 1979.

## Chapter 10   Morality Wars

Epigraph: "Holy Mass at the Logan Circle, Homily of His Holiness, John Paul II, Philadelphia, Wednesday, October 3, 1979," The Holy See, https:// www.vatican.va/content/john-paul-ii/en/homilies/1979/documents/hf_jp -ii_hom_19791003_logan-circle-philadelphia.html.
 1  John Dart and Russell Chandler, "U.S Catholics Respond With Surprise, Joy at Choice of Pontiff: His Anticommunism, Ties to the West Cited," *Los Angeles Times,* October 17, 1978.
 2  Joseph Cardinal Ratzinger, "Instruction on Certain Aspects of the 'Theology of Liberation' . . . Given at Rome, at the Sacred Congregation for the Doctrine of the Faith, on August 6, 1984, the Feast of the Transfiguration of Our Lord," The Holy See, https://www.vatican.va /roman_curia/congregations/cfaith/documents/rc_con_cfaith_doc _19840806_theology-liberation_en.html.
 3  "Holy Mass at the Logan Circle."
 4  For example, *The Living Bible* attempted to make Genesis more accessible. As such, rather than the commanding King James opening, "In the beginning, God created the heavens and the earth," it offered the more approachable, "When God began creating the heavens and the earth . . ." *The Living Bible* (Carol Stream, IL: Tyndale House Publish- ers, 1972), https://files.tyndale.com/thpdata/firstchapters/978-1-4143 -7857-2.pdf; *The Way: An Illustrated Edition of the Living Bible* (Carol Stream, IL: Tyndale House Publishers, 1973).
 5  "Radio station manager McClatchy said he believed the current growth in religious broadcasting stems from the youthful Jesus movement of a few years back." Kenneth F. Bunting, "Christian Movement Reaches Millions on Air Waves," *Los Angeles Times,* January 7, 1979.
 6  See, for example, Myev Alexandra Reeves, "A New Purpose: Rick Warren, the Megachurch Movement, and Early Twenty-First Century American Evangelical Discourse" (Master's thesis, Miami University, 2009), http://rave.ohiolink.edu/etdc/view?acc_num=miami1247428515.
 7  Bunting, "Christian Movement Reaches Millions on Air Waves."

8  John Dart, "'New Face' Emerging in Protestant Fundamentalism," *Los Angeles Times*, October 13, 1979.
9  "California Proposition 6, Ban on Lesbian and Gay Teachers Initiative (1978)," *Ballotpedia*, https://ballotpedia.org/California_Proposition_6,_Ban_on_Lesbian_and_Gay_Teachers_Initiative_(1978).
10  Russel Chandler, "Lobby Seeks 'Born-Again' Vote: Pasadena Group Aiming at Conservatives," *Los Angeles Times*, August 5, 1979.
11  John Van Gieson, "30,000 Rally for Decency," *Washington Post*, March 24, 1969.
12  Mike Royko, "Anita Crusades for Greenbacks (Orangebacks?)," *Los Angeles Times*, September 5, 1979.
13  Jon Nordheimer, "Miami Homosexuals See a Victory despite Defeat of Antibias Law," *New York Times*, December 28, 1977.
14  Terry Rubenstein, "Gay Rights—a March," *Baltimore Sun*, October 12, 1979; Courtland Milloy and Loretta Tofani, "Gay Rights Rally at the Monument," *Washington Post*, October 15, 1979.
15  Eileen Orgintz, "Schlafly Disciples Sharpen Their Political Skills," *Chicago Tribune*, October 14, 1979.
16  Renata Adler, "Screen: 'Green Berets' as Viewed by John Wayne," *New York Times*, June 20, 1968.
17  Roger Ebert, *"Apocalypse Now,"* RogerEbert.com, November 28, 1999, https://www.rogerebert.com/reviews/great-movie-apocalypse-now-1979; Roger Ebert, "How Do They Get to Be That Way?," RogerEbert.com, June 6, 2010, https://www.rogerebert.com/roger-ebert/how-do-they-get-to-be-that-way.
18  Gene Siskel, "A Profound, Chilling Foray into the Chaos and Horrors of War," *Chicago Tribune*, March 9, 1979.
19  Vincent Canby, "Blue Collar Epic," *New York Times*, December 15, 1978.
20  Weiss, *Double Play*, 403.
21  Weiss, 411–416.
22  Weiss, 411–416.
23  Weiss, 411–416.
24  Weiss, 411–416.
25  "Homosexuals' Parade Marks 10th Year of Right Drive," *New York Times*, June 25, 1979; Jo Thomas, "75,000 March in Capital in Drive to Support Homosexual Rights," *New York Times*, October 15, 1979.

## Chapter 11   A Shifting Chessboard

Epigraph: Zbigniew Brzezinski quoted in "United States Policy on the Khmer Rouge Regime, 1975–1979," Yale University Genocide Studies Program, accessed August 17, 2022, https://gsp.yale.edu/case-studies/cambodian-genocide-program/us-involvement/united-states-policy-khmer

-rouge-regime-1975. See also Grant Evans and Kelvin Rowley, *Red Brotherhood at War: Vietnam, Cambodia, and Laos since 1975*, rev. ed. (London: Verso, 1990).

1 Elizabeth Becker, "Cambodia: A Look at Border War with Vietnam: Artillery Thumps on Cambodia-Vietnam Border," *Washington Post*, December 27, 1978; "China Charges Viet Is Now Cuba of Asia," *Chicago Tribune*, December 26, 1978; Kevin Doyle, "Vietnam's Forgotten Cambodian War," *BBC*, September 14, 2014, https://www.bbc.com/news/world-asia-29106034.

2 James Carter, "How Close, Exactly, Were Russia and China to Nuclear War?," March 3, 2021, China Project, https://thechinaproject.com/2021/03/03/how-close-exactly-were-russia-and-china-to-nuclear-war/.

3 "New Development in Sino-Iranian Friendly Relations—Chairman Hua Visits Iran," *Peking Review* 21, no. 36 (September 8, 1978), in MIA, https://www.marxists.org/subject/china/peking-review/1978/PR1978-36.pdf.

4 "Hanoi's Bellicose Bleating," *Peking Review* 22, no. 1 (January 5, 1979), in MIA, https://www.marxists.org/subject/china/peking-review/1979/PR1979-01.pdf.

5 "Hanoi's Bellicose Bleating."

6 "Hanoi's Bellicose Bleating."

7 "Hanoi's Bellicose Bleating."

8 "United States Policy on the Khmer Rouge Regime, 1975–1979." See also Evans and Rowley, *Red Brotherhood at War*.

9 "The Cowboy-Hat and 'Deng Whirlwind'—The First Visit to the United States by a Leader of New China," *Global Times*, July 20, 2021, https://www.globaltimes.cn/page/202107/1229100.shtml.

10 "The Cowboy-Hat and 'Deng Whirlwind'"; John F. Burns, "Chinese Find It Hard to Say Nice Things about Their Former Ally, Hanoi," *New York Times*, May 5, 1985; Lee Lescaze, "Peking and Hanoi Teach Each Other a Lesson," *Washington Post*, March 18, 1979.

11 Minnie Chan, "Border War with Vietnam a Lingering Wound for China's Forgotten Soldiers," February 17, 2019.

12 "Frontier Forces Counter-Attack Vietnamese Aggressors," *Peking Review* 22, no. 8 (February 23, 1979), 3, in MIA, https://www.marxists.org/subject/china/peking-review/1979/PR1979-08.pdf.

13 Xiaoming Zhang, *Deng Xiaoping's Long War: The Military Conflict between China and Vietnam, 1979–1991* (Chapel Hill: University of North Carolina Press, 2015), 214.

14 "New Jewels in Grenada," *New York Times*, March 20, 1979; Peter Noel, "Grenada PM, Did He Tell It Like It Is?," *New York Amsterdam News*, October 20, 1979.

15 Leonard Greenwood, "As Strikers Demand Somoza Quit: Troops Patrol Streets in Nicaragua," *Los Angeles Times*, January 28, 1978.

16  James Nelson Goodsell, "Nicaragua: The Guerillas Become the Governors," *Christian Science Monitor*, August 3, 1979; Alan Riding, "Somoza Retires 100 Senior Officers amid Signs His Resignation Nears," *New York Times*, July 17, 1979; Cynthia Gorney, "Somoza Is Assassinated in Paraguay," *Washington Post*, September 18, 1980; David E. Rosenbaum, "US Gives Asylum to Some Deposed Leaders, but Not All," *New York Times*, December 9, 1979.

17  Karen DeYoung, "El Salvador's New Junta Troubled by Same Unrest as Ousted President," *Washington Post*, October 28, 1979.

18  Slogan is from Ernesto Che Guevara, *Guerilla Warfare*, ed., Brian Loveman and Thomas M. Davies (Manchester: Manchester University Press, 1986), 407.

19  William Chapman, "South Korea Confirms Assassination of Park," *Washington Post*, October 29, 1979; "Park Chung-Hee, 1917–1979," Wilson Center Digital Archive, accessed July 9, 2023, https://digitalarchive.wilsoncenter.org/people/park-chung-hee.

20  William Borders, "British Tory Is Slain in Parliament Yard," *New York Times*, March 31, 1979; Stephen Kelly, "The Life and Death of British Spy Turned Politician Airey Neave," *RTÉ.ie*, March 28, 2019, https://www.rte.ie/brainstorm/2019/0328/1039118-the-life-and-death-of-british-spy-turned-politician-airey-neave/.

21  James Mittelman, "Apartheid, Mighty but Doomed," *New York Times*, March 18, 1979.

22  William Borders, "Rhodesian Guerillas Agree to Britain's Cease-Fire Plan," *New York Times*, December 18, 1979; "Zimbabwe," South African History Online, accessed August 21, 2022, https://www.sahistory.org.za/place/zimbabwe.

## Chapter 12   The Looming 1980s

Epigraph: Jimmy Carter, "Energy and the National Goals—A Crisis of Confidence," July 15, 1979, American Rhetoric, https://www.americanrhetoric.com/speeches/jimmycartercrisisofconfidence.htm.

1  Joseph J. Collins, "The Soviet Invasion of Afghanistan: Methods, Motives, and Ramifications," *Naval War College Review* 33, no. 6 (November–December 1980): 53–62.

2  Michael T. Kaufman, "No Light at End of the Tunnel for Russians in Afghanistan," *New York Times*, September 23, 1979.

3  Deepak Tripathi, *Breeding Ground: Afghanistan and the Origins of Islamist Terrorism* (Lincoln: University of Nebraska Press, 2011), 50–54; Christopher Solomon, "40 Years after His Death, Hafizullah Amin Casts a Long Shadow in Afghanistan," *The Diplomat*, December 31, 2019, https://thediplomat.com/2019/12/40-years-after-his-death-hafizullah-amin-casts-a-long-shadow-in-afghanistan/.

4   Gregory Feifer, "Russia's 'Great Gamble': Lessons from Afghanistan," January 8, 2009, https://www.npr.org/2009/01/08/99090399/russias -great-gamble-lessons-from-afghanistan.

5   Tripathi, *Breeding Ground*, 41–49.

6   Vincent Jauvert, "Les Révélations d'un Ancien Conseiller de Carter," *Le Nouvel Observateur*, January 15–21, 1998, 76, cited in Julie Lowenstein, "US Foreign Policy and the Soviet-Afghan War: A Revisionist History" (2016), Harvey M. Applebaum '59 Award Essay 9, https://elischolar .library.yale.edu/applebaum_award/9, p. 16.

7   Jauvert, "Les Révélations," 76.

8   Kaufman, "No Light at End of the Tunnel."

9   Fred Weir, "A War the US 'Can't Win,'" *South China Morning Post* (Hong Kong), October 14, 2001.

10  Weir, "A War the US 'Can't Win.'"

11  Jimmy Carter, "Address to the Nation on the Soviet Invasion of Afghanistan," January 4, 1980, American Presidency Project, https:// www.presidency.ucsb.edu/documents/address-the-nation-the-soviet -invasion-afghanistan.

12  "Barnett Rubin on the Soviet Invasion of Afghanistan and the Rise of the Taliban," Asia Society, accessed August 7, 2022, https://asiasociety .org/barnett-rubin-soviet-invasion-afghanistan-and-rise-taliban.

13  Oswald Johnston, "Reality and Mr. Carter," *Guardian*, December 28, 1977.

14  "Carter and Human Rights, 1977–1981," Office of the Historian, accessed August 14, 2022, https://history.state.gov/milestones/1977 -1980/human-rights.

15  "Ronald Reagan on the Unrest on College Campuses, 1967," Gilder Lehman Institute of American History, History Resources, https:// www.gilderlehrman.org/history-resources/spotlight-primary-source /ronald-reagan-unrest-college-campuses-1967.

16  Rebecca J. Rosen, "Video: Ronald Reagan's Press Conference after 'Bloody Thursday,'" *Atlantic*, February 24, 2014, https://www .theatlantic.com/politics/archive/2014/02/video-ronald-reagans-press -conference-after-bloody-thursday/284045/.

17  "Ronald Regan's 1980 Neshoba County Fair Speech," *Neshoba Democrat*, April 8, 2021, https://neshobademocrat.com/stories/ronald -reagans-1980-neshoba-county-fair-speech,49123.

18  "Ronald Reagan's Announcement for Presidential Candidacy, January 13, 1979," Ronald Reagan Presidential Library and Museum, https://www.reaganlibrary.gov/archives/speech/ronald-reagans -announcement-presidential-candidacy-1979.

19  For more, see Greg Thielman, "The Missile Gap Myth and Its Progeny," Arms Control Association, accessed December 25, 2022, https://www .armscontrol.org/act/2011-05/missile-gap-myth-its-progeny.

20 "Best Sellers," *New York Times*, June 24, 1979, https://www.nytimes
.com/1979/06/24/archives/best-sellers-fiction.html.
21 Judy Klemesrud, "Behind the Bestsellers: Gen. Sir John Hackett,"
*New York Times*, May 27, 1979.
22 Thomas Lask, "New Thriller by Forsyth Will Come Out in March,"
*New York Times*, June 11, 1979.
23 Geoffrey Godsell, "Moscow's Temptation in Turbulent Iran," *Christian
Science Monitor*, January 15, 1979.
24 Frederic A. Moritz, "China, Soviets, US: All Face Hard Choices,"
*Christian Science Monitor*, February 20, 1979.
25 Robert Cross, "The '70s: The Age of Depletion," *Chicago Tribune*,
December 9, 1979.

## Conclusion

1 Paul Hoffman, "Pope, in an Appeal on Peace Day, Warns of Effects of a
Nuclear War," *New York Times*, January 2, 1980.
2 Abeeb Khalid, *Islam after Communism: Religion and Politics in Central
Asia* (Berkeley: University of California Press, 2007), 116.
3 See Rush Doshi, *The Long Game: China's Grand Strategy to Displace
American Order* (New York: Oxford University Press, 2021).

## Coda

1 "What Really Happened in the 1989 Tiananmen Square Protests,"
Amnesty International, May 18, 2023, https://www.amnesty.org.uk
/china-1989-tiananmen-square-protests-demonstration-massacre.
2 See, for example, Peter Baker, "A Four-Decade Secret: One Man's Story
of Sabotaging Carter's Re-Election," *New York Times*, March 18, 2023.
3 "Iran: Violations of Human Rights 1987–1990," Amnesty International,
December 1, 1990, https://www.amnesty.org/en/documents/mde13/021
/1990/en/.
4 "U.S. Involvement in the 1980s Iran-Iraq War: America's Haphazard
Extension of Gulf Insecurity," *Yale Review of International Studies*
(December 2019), http://yris.yira.org/comments/2729; "Iran-Iraq War,"
*History.com*, July 13, 2021, https://www.history.com/topics/middle-east
/iran-iraq-war.
5 Lara Jakes Jordan and Matt Apuzzo, "After Suicide, Feds Consider
Closing Anthrax Case," *ABC News*, August 2, 2008, https://web.archive
.org/web/20080807033754/https://abcnews.go.com/TheLaw/wireStory
?id=5502344.
6 Katelyn Harris, "Forty Years of Falling Manufacturing Employment,"
*Beyond the Numbers* 9, no. 16 (November 2020), https://www.bls.gov
/opub/btn/volume-9/forty-years-of-falling-manufacturing-employment
.htm; Darrell M. West and Christian Lansang, "Global Manufacturing

Scorecard: How the US Compares to 18 Other Nations," Brookings Institute, July 10, 2018, https://www.brookings.edu/research/global-manufacturing-scorecard-how-the-us-compares-to-18-other-nations/.

7 "Bob Avakian Demands Political Refugee Status in France," *Revolutionary Worker* 2, no. 45 (March 20, 1981), in MIA, https://www.marxists.org/history/erol/periodicals/revolutionary-worker/rw-97.pdf.

8 "This Day in History, November 3, 1979," *History.com*, accessed November 8, 2022, https://www.history.com/this-day-in-history/communists-and-klansmen-clash-in-greensboro.

9 "Communist Workers Party/New Democratic Movement," in MIA, accessed May 7, 2023, https://www.marxists.org/history/erol/ncm-7/index.htm#cwp.

10 John L. Puckett, "MOVE on Osage Avenue," West Philadelphia Collaborative History, accessed February 11, 2023, https://collaborativehistory.gse.upenn.edu/stories/move-osage-avenue.

11 Don Terry, "Philadelphia Held Liable for Firebomb Fatal to 11," *New York Times*, June 25, 1996.

12 For more, see Burrough, *Days of Rage*; Ellen Frankfort, *Kathy Boudin, and the Dance of Death* (New York: Stein and Day, 1983); and Char Adams, "Tupac Shakur's Stepfather Reflects on Freedom after 35 Years Behind Bars," *NBC News*, January 31, 2023, https://www.nbcnews.com/news/nbcblk/tupac-shakurs-stepfather-finds-freedom-35-years-prison-rcna68195.

13 See, for example, Steve Chapman, "The Vietnam Syndrome: How We Lost It and Why We Need It," *Chicago Tribune*, September 20, 2017, https://www.chicagotribune.com/columns/steve-chapman/ct-perspec-chapman-vietnam-syndrome-afghanistan-20170921-story.html.

# Bibliography

Abrahamian, Ervand. *A History of Modern Iran*. Cambridge: Cambridge University Press, 2008.

———. *Iran Between Two Revolutions*. Princeton, NJ: Princeton University Press, 1982.

Armstrong, Gregory. *The Dragon Has Come*. New York: Harper Row, 1974.

Axworthy, Michael. *Revolutionary Iran: A History of the Islamic Republic*. New York: Oxford University Press, 2013.

Ayers, William. *Fugitive Days: A Memoir*. Boston: Beacon Press, 2001.

Barron, John. *Operation Solo: The FBI's Man in the Kremlin*. Washington, DC: Regnery Publishing, 2013.

Borstelmann, Thomas. *The 1970s: A New Global History from Civil Rights to Economic Inequality*. Princeton: Princeton University Press, 2013.

Briton, Jean-Charles. *US Officials and the Fall of the Shah: Some Safe Contraction Interpretations*. Lanham, MD: Lexington Books, 2010.

Brzezinski, Zbigniew. *Grand Chessboard: American Primacy and Its Geostrategic Imperatives*. New York: Basic Books, 1998.

Burrough, Bryan. *Days of Rage: America's Radical Underground, the FBI, and the Forgotten Age of Revolutionary Violence*. New York: Penguin, 2015.

Caryl, Christian. *Strange Rebels: 1979 and the Birth of the 21st Century*. New York: Basic Books, 2013.

Chard, Daniel. *Nixon's War at Home*. Chapel Hill: University of North Carolina Press, 2021.

Coll, Steve. *Ghost Wars: The Secret History of the CIA, Afghanistan, and Bin Laden, from the Soviet Invasion to September 10, 2001*. New York: Penguin, 2011.

Cowie, Jefferson. *Stayin' Alive: The 1970s and the Last Days of the Working Class*. New York: New Press, 2010.

Didion, Joan. *The White Album*. New York: Simon and Schuster, 1979.

Dobbs, Michael. *One Minute to Midnight: Kennedy, Khrushchev and Castro on the Brink of Nuclear War*. New York: Vintage 2009.

Donner, Frank. *Protectors of the Privilege: Red Squads and Police Repression in Urban America*. Berkeley: University of California Press, 1990.

Doshi, Rush. *The Long Game: China's Grand Strategy to Displace American Order*. New York: Oxford University Press, 2021.

Durden-Smith, Jo. *Who Killed George Jackson? Fantasies, Paranoia, and the Revolution*. New York: Knopf, 1976.

Eckstein, Arthur M. *Bad Moon Rising: How the Weathermen Beat the FBI and Lost the Revolution*. New Haven, CT: Yale University Press, 2016.

Faludi, Susan. *Backlash: The Undeclared War Against American Women*. New York: Crown, 1991.

Farber, David, and Beth Bailey. *America in the Seventies*. Lawrence: University of Kansas Press, 2004.

Foner, Eric. *Give Me Liberty!: An American History*. New York: W. W. Norton, 2009.

Forsyth, Fredrick. *The Devil's Alternative*. London: Hutchinson, 1979.

Frankfort, Ellen. *Kathy Boudin and the Dance of Death*. New York: Stein and Day, 1983.

Frum, David. *How We Got Here: The 70's: The Decade That Brought You Modern Life, for Better or Worse*. New York: Basic Books, 2000.

Gallagher, Carol. *America Ground Zero: The Secret Nuclear War*. New York: Random House 1994.

Garrow, David. *The FBI and Martin Luther King, Jr.: From Solo to Memphis*. New York: W. W. Norton, 1981.

Gilbert, Pat. *Passion Is a Fashion: The Real Story of the Clash*. London: Aurum Press, 2005.

Golub, Philip S. *Power, Profit and Prestige: A History of American Imperial Expansion*. London: Pluto Press 2010.

Gray, Marcus. *The Clash: Return of the Last Gang in Town*. Milwaukee: Hal Leonard, 2004.

Gray, Mike, and Ira Rosen. *The Warning: Accident at Three Mile Island*. New York: W. W. Norton, 1982.

Guinn, Jeff. *The Road to Jonestown: Jim Jones and His Peoples Temple*. New York: Simon and Schuster, 2017.

Haas, Jeff. *The Assassination of Fred Hampton: How the FBI and the Chicago Police Murdered a Black Panther*. Chicago: Lawrence Hill Books, 2011.

Hackett, Sir John. *The Third World War: 1985*. New York: Macmillan, 1979.

Harvey, David. *A Brief History of Neoliberalism*. New York: Oxford University Press, 2005.

———. *A Companion to Capital*. Vol. 1. New York: Verso, 2010.

Higginbotham, Adam. *Midnight in Chernobyl: The Untold Story of the World's Greatest Nuclear Disaster*. New York: Simon and Schuster, 2020.

Hobsbawm, Eric. *The Age of Extremes: A History of the World, 1914–1991.* New York: Vintage 1996.

Hoffman, David. *The Dead Hand: The Untold Story of the Cold War Arms Race and Its Dangerous Legacy.* New York, Doubleday, 2009.

Jacobs, Meg. *Panic at the Pump: The Energy Crisis and the Transformation of American Politics in the 1970s.* New York: Hill and Wang, 2016.

Jacobs, Ron. *The Way the Wind Blew: A History of the Weather Underground.* New York: Verso Books, 1997.

Jenkins, Philip. *Decade of Nightmares: The End of the Sixties and the Making of Eighties America.* New York: Oxford University Press, 2006.

Khalid, Abeeb. *Islam after Communism: Religion and Politics in Central Asia.* Berkeley: University of California Press, 2006.

Leonard, Aaron J., and Conor A. Gallagher. *Heavy Radicals: The FBI's Secret War on America's Maoists.* Rev. ed. Winchester, UK: Zero Books, 2022.

———. *A Threat of the First Magnitude: FBI Counterintelligence and Infiltration.* London: Repeater Books, 2017.

MacLean, Nancy. *The American Women's Movement, 1945–2000: A Brief History with Documents.* New York: Bedford/Saint Martins, 2009.

Mangold, Tom, and Jeff Goldberg. *Plague Wars: The Terrifying Reality of Biological Warfare.* New York: St. Martin's Griffin, 1999.

Marx, Karl. *Capital.* Vol. 1. New York: International Publishers, 1975.

McCormick, Thomas J. *America's Half-Century: United States Foreign Policy in the Cold War.* Baltimore: Johns Hopkins University Press, 1989.

Meisner, Maurice. *The Deng Xiaoping Era: An Inquiry into the Fate of Chinese Socialism, 1978–1994.* New York: Hill and Wang, 1996.

Morris, Stephen J. *Why Vietnam Invaded Cambodia: Political Culture and the Causes of War.* Stanford, CA: Stanford University Press, 1999.

Neumann, Tracy. *Remaking the Rust Belt: The Postindustrial Transformation of North America.* Philadelphia: University of Pennsylvania Press, 2016.

Odinga, Sekou, Dhoruba Bin Wahad, and Jamal Joseph. *Look for Me in the Whirlwind: From the Panther 21 to 21st-Century Revolutions.* Oakland, CA: PM Press, 2017.

Onaci, Edward. *Free the Land: The Republic of New Afrika and the Pursuit of a Black Nation-State.* Chapel Hill: University of North Carolina Press, 2020.

Plohky, Serhii. *Nuclear Folly: A History of the Cuban Missile Crisis.* New York: W. W. Norton, 2021.

Rashid, Ahmed. *Descent into Chaos: The US and the Disaster in Pakistan, Afghanistan, and Central Asia.* New York: Penguin, 2009.

Roberts, Lawrence. *May Day 1971: A White House at War, a Revolt in the Streets, and the Untold History of America's Biggest Mass Arrest.* Boston: Mariner Books, 2020.

Rudd, Mark. *Underground: My Life with SDS and the Weathermen*. New York: HarperCollins, 2009.

Samuelson, Robert. *The Great Inflation: The Past and Future of American Affluence*. New York: Random House, 2010.

Smil, Vaclav. *Made in the USA: The Rise and Retreat of American Manufacturing*. Cambridge, MA: MIT Press, 2013.

Teiwes, Fredrick C. *The End of the Maoist Era*. Armonk, NY: M. E. Sharpe, 2007.

Tripathi, Deepak. *Breeding Ground: Afghanistan and the Origins of Islamist Terrorism*. Lincoln: University of Nebraska Press, 2011.

Tung, Jerry. *The Socialist Road*. New York: Cesar Cause Publishers, 1981.

Vonnegut, Kurt. *Jailbird*. New York: Dell Publishing, 1979.

Waller, Signe. *Love and Revolution: A Political Memoir*. Lanham, MD: Rowman and Littlefield, 2002.

Weather Underground. *Prairie Fire: The Politics of Revolutionary Anti-Imperialism*. San Francisco: Communications Co., 1974.

Weiss, Mike. *Double Play: The San Francisco City Hall Killings*. Boston: Addison Wesley Publishing, 1984.

Westad, Odd. *The Global Cold War: Third World Interventions and the Making of Our Times*. New York: Oxford University Press, 2005.

Wheaton, Elizabeth. *Codename Greenkill: The 1979 Greensboro Killings*. Athens: University of Georgia Press, 1987.

Winant, Gabriel. *The Next Shift: The Fall of Industry and the Rise of Health Care in Rust Belt America*. Cambridge, MA: Harvard University Press, 2021.

Zhang, Xiaoming. *Deng Xiaoping's Long War: The Military Conflict between China and Vietnam, 1979–1991*. Chapel Hill: University of North Carolina Press, 2015.

# Filmography

Ashby, Hal, director. *Being There*. Beverly Hills, CA, United Artists, 1979.

Ashby, Hal, director. *Coming Home*. Beverly Hills, CA: United Artists, 1978.

Badham, John, director. *War Games*. Beverly Hills, CA: United Artists, 1983.

Carlino, Lewis John, director. *The Great Santini*. Burbank, CA: Warner Brothers, 1979.

Cimino, Michael, director. *The Deer Hunter*. Universal City, CA: Universal Pictures, 1978.

Coppola, Francis, director. *Apocalypse Now*. Universal City, CA: Universal, 1979.

Davidson, Keif, director. *Meltdown: Three Mile Island*. Los Angeles, CA: Netflix, 2022.

Davis, Peter, director. *Hearts and Minds*. Burbank, CA: Rainbow Releasing/Warner Bros., 1974.

Dwan, Allan, director. *Sands of Iwo Jima*. Republic Pictures, 1949.

Henzell, Perry, director. *The Harder They Come*. Atlanta, GA: New World Pictures, 1972.

*History's Mysteries: The Greensboro Massacre*. New York: A&E Television Networks, 2000.

Letts, Don, director. *The Clash: Westway to the World*. London: 3DD Entertainment, 2000.

Meyer, Nicholas, director *The Day After*. Burbank, CA: ABC Motion Pictures, 1983.

Milius, John, director. *Red Dawn*. Beverly Hills, CA: MGM/UA Entertainment, 1984.

Miller, George, director. *Mad Max*. Burbank, CA: Warner Brothers, 1979.

Potenza, Anthony, and Danny Goldberg, directors. *No Nukes*. Burbank, CA: Warner Brothers, 1980.

Romero, George, director. *Dawn of the Dead*. Beverly Hills, CA: United Artists, 1979.

Sucher, Joel, director. *Red Squad*. Brooklyn: NY, Pacific Street Films, 1972.

Waller, Dahvi, creator, *Mrs. America*. Burbank, CA: HULU, 2020.

Wayne, John, and Ray Kellogg, directors. *The Green Berets*. Warner Bros-Seven Arts, 1968.

Wyler, William, director. *The Best Years of Our Lives*. Samuel Goldwyn Productions 1946.

Zeiger, David, director, *Sir! No Sir!* Los Angeles, CA: Displaced Films, 2005.

Zucker, Adam, director. *Greensboro: Closer to the Truth*. Ann Arbor, MI: Filmmakers Library, 2009.

# Selected Discography

Bee Gees. *Saturday Night Fever*. RSO, 1977.

Browne, Jackson. *Lawyers in Love*. Asylum, 1983.

Buzzcocks. *Spiral Scratch* (EP). New Hormones, 1977.

The Clash. *The Clash*. CBS, 1977.

———. *Give 'Em Enough Rope*. Epic, 1978.

———. *London Calling*. Epic, 1979.

Cliff, Jimmy. *The Harder They Come Soundtrack*. Island, 1972.

Doobie Brothers. *Takin' It to the Streets*. Warner Brothers, 1976.

Dylan, Bob. *Blood on the Tracks*. Columbia, 1975.

———. *Desire*. Columbia, 1976.

———. *Live 1975: The Rolling Thunder Review*. Columbia, 2002.

———. *Slow Train Coming*. Columbia, 1979.

Eagles. *The Long Run*. Asylum, 1979.

Fleetwood Mac. *Tusk*. Warner Brothers, 1979.

Harrison, George. *Concert for Bangladesh*. Apple, 1971.

Juluka. *Universal Men*. CBS, 1979.

Marley, Bob. *Survival*. Island/Tuff Gong, 1979.

Parker, Graham, and the Rumour. *Squeezing Out Sparks*. Arista, 1979.

Pop, Iggy. "I'm Bored" (UK single). Arista, 1979.

Price, Lloyd. "Stagger Lee" (single). ABC Paramount, 1958.

Ramones. *Ramones*. Sire Records, 1976.

The Rulers. "Wrong 'Em Boyo" (single). Direct Records, 1967.

Scott-Heron, Gil, and Brian Jackson. *Bridges*. Arista, 1977.

Sex Pistols. *Never Mind the Bollocks: Here's the Sex Pistols*. EMI, 1977.

The Specials. *The Specials*. 2 Tone, 1979.

Springsteen, Bruce. *Born to Run*. Columbia, 1976.

———. *Darkness on the Edge of Town*. Columbia, 1978.

———. *The River*. Columbia, 1980.

Springsteen, Bruce, and the East Street Band. *The Legendary 1979 No Nukes Concerts*. Legacy Records, 2021.

Summer, Donna. "Macarthur Park" (single). Casablanca Records, 1978.

Timbuk 3. *Greetings from Timbuk 3*. I.R.S., 1986.

Tosh, Peter. *Equal Rights*. Columbia, 1977.

———. *Mystic Man*. Rolling Stone Records, 1979.

Various Artists. *Grease: The Original Soundtrack from the Motion Picture*. Asylum, 1978.

Various Artists. *No Nukes*. Asylum, 1979.

Vince Taylor Vine and His Playboys. "Brand New Cadillac" (single). Parlaphone, 1959.

The Who. *Who Are You*. Polydor/MCA, 1978.

# Index

Note: Page numbers in italics refer to figures.

*China Syndrome, The* (film), 31–33
Christianity: broadcasting, 124–126;
   moral values of, 122, 123, 125–126;
   popular methods, 123
Christian right, 123
*Christian Science Monitor,* 151–152
Chrysler Corporation, 53–54
Chrysler Loan Guarantee Act, 53
Church Committee, 5, 92
"Clampdown" (song), 117
Clapton, Eric, 115, 186n19
Clark, Judith, 160
Clark, Mark, 96
Clash (rock band), 6; albums of,
   14–15, 116–118; photo of, *116*
Cleaver, Eldridge, 65–66, 82, 114
Cliff, Jimmy, 118
Clinton Correctional Facility escape,
   83–84
coal mining, 175n25
Coder, Ry, 34
Cold War, 2, 134, 152
Cole, Arthur, 47
*Coming Home* (film), 127–128
Communist Party USA (CPUSA), 92,
   95, 182n9–10
Communist Workers Party (CWP):
   "Death to the Klan" rally, 72–73;
   decline of, 159; events in China
   Grove, 71–72; radical activism of,
   70, 71
computer technology: impact on job
   market, 50–51
Concerned Relatives, 10
Cone Mill plant in Greensboro, 70
Conrad, Joseph, 128
Coppola, Francis Ford, 128
Counterintelligence Program
   (COINTELPRO), 89, 92, 95,
   182n9–10
Creswell, James, 33
Crosby, Stills & Nash (CSN), 34
Cross, Robert, 152
Cuban Missile Crisis, 35, 150

Dade County ordinance, 125
Dahl, Steve, 107–108
"Dancing in the Street" (song), 112
*Darkness on the Edge of Town* (album),
   112
Davis, Rennie, 67
"Days of Rage" demonstration, 79
DC-10 crashes in Chicago, 117
"Deep Throat," 90
*Deer Hunter, The* (film), 129
deindustrialization, 47–49, 174n13
Deng, Xiaoping: criticism of, 57;
   demonstration against, 159;
   economic policy of, 60; on human
   rights in China, 62; Jiang Qing
   and, 60–61; meeting with Carter,
   64, 69; political career of, 55–56, 57,
   58; revision of Mao's policies,
   60–62; as *Time*'s "Man of the
   Year," 64; U.S. Maoists and, 68;
   visit to the U.S., xvii, 4, *63*, 136
Dern, Bruce, 127
détente policy, 5, 35–36
*Devil's Alternative, The* (Forsyth), 151
Dillinger, David, 67
Disco Demolition Night, 107–109
disco music, 14, 108–109
Dohrn, Bernardine, 80, 81
*Do It!: Scenarios of the Revolution*
   (Rubin), 66
Doobie Brothers (rock band), 34
Dotson, Floyd, 81
Douglas, Michael, 32
"Downpressor Man" (song), 119
Dylan, Bob, 113–114

Eagle Forum, 126
Earl, Samuel D., 43–44
Ebert, Roger, 128–129
Egypt, 6, 15
Ellsberg, Daniel, 67
El Salvador, 134, 139, 153, 160
energy crisis, 45
English Beat (band), 116

Rally for Decency, 125
Ramones (rock band), 6, 14
Ramp, James, 75
Rastafarianism, 118
Reagan, Ronald: arms race, 154;
conservative view of, 149; economic
policy, 52, 149; Eldridge Cleaver
and, 65–66; foreign policy,
149–150, 153–154, 160; Iran hostage
crisis and, 157; pardon of Felt and
Miller, 106; presidential election,
148, 153; on United States' place in
the world, 149–150
Red Army Faction (RAF), 86
reggae music, 118–119
religious broadcasting, 187n5
Republic of New Afrika (RNA), 81
Revell, Oliver "Buck," 85, 86
Revolutionary Communist Party
(RCP): anti-Deng demonstration
of, 68–69, 71; crisis of, xvi, 67; FBI
investigation of, 67–68, 92–93;
formation of, 2; slogan of, 68,
179n27
Revolutionary Communist Youth
Brigade, xvi
Revolutionary Student Brigade
(RSB), 67
Revolutionary Union. See Revolu-
tionary Communist Party, USA
(RCP)
"Revolution Will Not Be Televised,
The" (song), 34
Rhodesia. See Zimbabwe
Rison, Tyron, 83–84
"River, The" (song), 34
Riverfront Stadium in Cincinnati, 109
Rizzo, Frank, 74
Roberts, Gene, 82
Robertson, Pat, 124
Robins, Terry, 78
Robinson, Stanley, 101, 103
Rock Against Racism (RAR)
movement, 116, 186n20

rock 'n' roll music, 3, 15, 107–108, 109,
111, 116
Rolling Stone (magazine), 108
Rolling Stones (rock band), 2, 15
Romero, Carlos Humberto, 139
Roosevelt, Kermit, 19, 20
Rosse, Nancy, 54
Rubin, Barnett, 147
Rubin, Jerry, 66
Rudd, Mark, 79–80
Rumour (rock band), 116
Ryan, David, 93
Ryan, Leo, 10

Sadat, Anwar, 6, 16
Safire, William, 38
SALT I and SALT II (Strategic Arms
Limitations Talks) agreements, 1,
35–36, 37, 125, 171n12, 171n14
Salvadoran Civil War, 5
Sampson, Will, 73
Sands of Iwo Jima (film), 127
San Francisco, CA: Castro District,
130; City Hall shooting, 8, 12–13,
129, 154; gay rights demonstrations,
129–131, 131; International Hotel
rally, 8–10, 9; photo outside of
City Hall, 131; right-wing violence
in, 8
Save Our Children fundraising card,
126
Schlafly, Phyllis, 125–126
Schwarzkopf, H. Norman, 19–20
Schwerner, Michael, 149
Scott-Heron, Gil, 6, 34
Seale, Bobby, 10
Seberg, Jean, 89
Senate committee hearing on
manufacturing, 46–47
Serratia marcescens, 40
700 Club, The (TV show), 124
Sex Pistols (punk rock band), 14
Shakur, Assata (a.k.a. Joanne
Chesimard), 82–83, 84, 160

## About the Author


AARON J. LEONARD is the author of *Heavy Radicals: The FBI's Secret War on America's Maoists*, *The Folk Singers and the Bureau*, and *Whole World in an Uproar: Music, Rebellion, and Repression 1955–1972*. He has a BA in social sciences and history magna cum laude from New York University. He lives in Los Angeles.